Editor
Mary S. Jones, M.A.

Editor in Chief
Karen J. Goldfluss, M.S. Ed.

Cover Artist
Barb Lorseyedi

Imaging
James Edward Grace
Craig Gunnell

Publisher
Mary D. Smith, M.S. Ed.

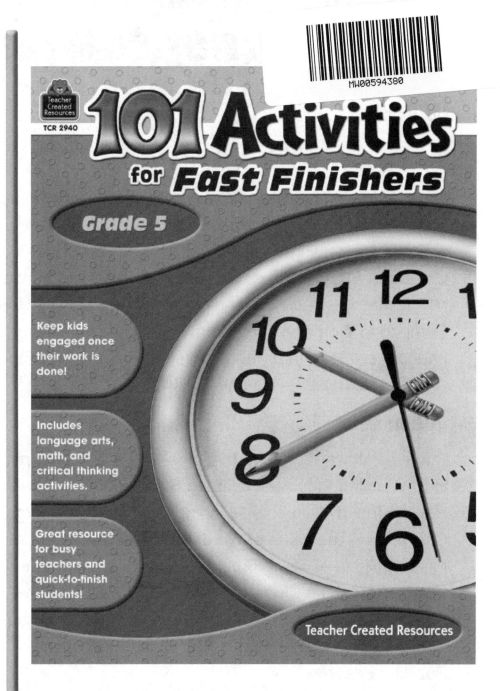

101 Activities for *Fast Finishers*

Grade 5

TCR 2940

Keep kids engaged once their work is done!

Includes language arts, math, and critical thinking activities.

Great resource for busy teachers and quick-to-finish students!

Teacher Created Resources

Teacher Created Resources
6421 Industry Way
Westminster, CA 92683
www.teachercreated.com

ISBN: 978-1-4206-2940-8

© 2011 Teacher Created Resources
Made in U.S.A.

Teacher Created Resources

TABLE OF CONTENTS

Introduction **3**

Lively Language Arts **4**

Letter Grid—Word Pairs—Mystery Words—Quick Words—Missing *Es*—
Blankity Blanks—Funny Verbs—Missing Vowels—Swap Shops—Synonyms—
Antonyms—Helping Verbs—Spell Well—Fronts and Backs—Missing
Creatures—Parts of Speech—Small Words—Arithmetic—Mixed-Up Meals—
Mix 'N Match—Multiple Meanings—Give Me a "C"—Homophones—
Compound Words—Which Word?—Fixing Errors—Transitions—Figurative
Language—Sequence—Big Ideas—A Pretend Election—Dance Fever—
An Unusual Inmate—Llamas—Tall Tales

Mind-Bender Math **39**

Square Pathways—Tricky Triangles—Sale Time—Symmetry—Math Terms A
to Z—Circling Around—Common Sides—Magic Squares—Totals—Number
Rows—Touchy Numbers—Finding Coordinates—Number Quiz—Sudoku
Challenge—The Value of Words—Addition Boxes—Coin Combinations—
Missing Signs—Picture Problem—Geometrical Challenge—What's the
End?—Follow the Clues—Four Signs—Wheel of Fun—Number Puzzle—
Answer Match—Multiplication Madness—Fred the Frog—Missing Integers—
Fraction Fun—Math Square—City Grid—Math Trivia—Calculated Story—
Puzzling Patterns

Beyond Brainy **74**

Body Parts—Odd One Out—Naming Fun—License Plates—Map Madness—
Match Up—Tantalizing Tiles—Reverse Words—Picture Sayings—Idioms—
When Is It?—Oxymorons—Favorite Teams—Letter Puzzle—Hidden Animals—
Word Chain—Hidden Meanings—Working with Codes—Changing Letters—
Car Rally—Around the Island—Step by Step—Colorful Puzzlers—
Boggle the Mind—The Big Race—Coded Message—Baseball Equations—
Word Winders—Presidential Puns—Geography Sandwiches—Highest Score

Answer Key **105**

INTRODUCTION

All students work at different speeds. Many take about the same amount of time to finish their work. Some are slower than others, and some are faster than others. You've probably been asked, "I'm done, what do I do now?" more times than you can count. But what's a teacher to do when one or more students finish early? The activity pages in *101 Activities for Fast Finishers* are the answer.

The 101 activities in this book focus on language arts, math, and critical thinking, and are divided as follows:

- Lively Language Arts (35 activities)
- Mind-Bender Math (35 activities)
- Beyond Brainy (31 activities)

Each activity has been labeled with an approximate amount of time that it will take students to complete. The estimated times range from 5 to 20 minutes. It is recommended that you copy, in advance, several pages representing the different times, and have them on hand to distribute, as needed. When a student asks you that famous "What do I do now?" question, a quick look at the clock will tell you which activity to give him or her. These activities will also be helpful to keep in your emergency substitute file as filler activities.

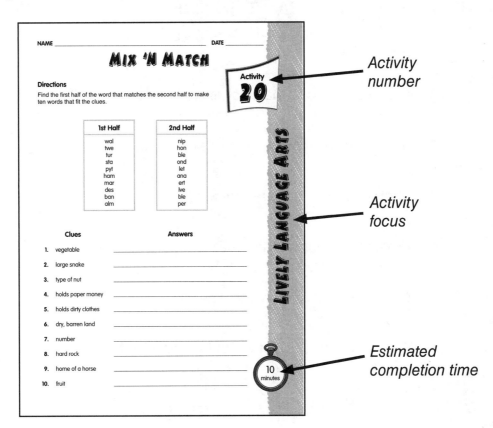

LETTER GRID

Directions

Look at the rows of letters in the grid below. Use them to answer the questions that follow.

LIVELY LANGUAGE ARTS

1	M	T	A	E	R	O
2	E	O	T	R	M	T
3	W	Y	X	B	Y	E
4	M	T	Q	P	X	T
5	V	Y	W	S	T	V
6	A	P	U	E	I	O

1. Which row contains the most letters that come after R in the alphabet? _____

2. What letter is always to the right of M in the grid? _____

3. What vowel occurs the most times? _____

4. Which row contains all the vowels? _____

5. Which rows contain only consonants? _____

6. Make four words using the first four letters in the first row.

_____

5 minutes

WORD PAIRS

Activity 2

Directions

If the words in the following pairs are similar (synonyms), write *S*. If they are opposite to each other (antonyms), write *A*. If they have no obvious connection, write *X*.

1.   straight   bent   _____

2.   buy   sell   _____

3.   plentiful   ample   _____

4.   old   table   _____

5.   summit   top   _____

6.   finish   end   _____

7.   sharp   new   _____

8.   sour   sweet   _____

9.   broad   wide   _____

10.   tall   silly   _____

11.   margin   edge   _____

12.   cease   stop   _____

13.   jewel   gem   _____

14.   strong   weak   _____

LIVELY LANGUAGE ARTS

5 minutes

MYSTERY WORDS

Directions

Can you figure out the mystery words below? First solve the smaller words using the clues given. Write the correct letter in the space to the right of each number. Then match that letter with the corresponding number in the mystery word to find out what the mystery word is.

LIVELY LANGUAGE ARTS

Clues:

1. grass around the house: 3____   2____   6____   9____

2. part of the foot: 1____   7____   7____   4____

3. what a mouse lives in: 1____   5____   3____   8____

4. the world's largest mammal: 6____   1____   2____   3____   8____

Mystery Word: ____ ____ ____ ____ ____ ____ ____ ____ ____
            1   2   3   4   5   6   7   8   9

Clues:

5. use sissors: 1____   8____   4____

6. applaud: 1____   6____   2____   9____

7. small, open boat: 1____   5____   3____   7____   10____

Mystery Word: ____ ____ ____ ____ ____ ____ ____ ____ ____ ____
            1   2   3   4   5   6   7   8   9   10

5
minutes

QUICK WORDS

Activity
4

Directions

In five minutes, how many words can you make using the letters in the box? Every word must contain the letter *E*.

E		M	N
		W	F
P	T	G	H
A	B	L	R

_____ _____

_____ _____

_____ _____

_____ _____

_____ _____ _____

_____ _____ _____

_____ _____ _____

_____ _____ _____

_____ _____ _____

_____ _____ _____

_____ _____ _____

_____ _____ _____

_____ _____ _____

LIVELY LANGUAGE ARTS

5
minutes

MISSING Es

Directions

Two *E*s are missing from each of these words. Can you put them back correctly?

1.   agl   (bird)   _____

2.   jwl   (precious stone)   _____

3.   fnc   (barrier)   _____

4.   gnral   (army rank)   _____

5.   nmy   (foe)   _____

6.   vlvt   (soft cloth)   _____

7.   prfct   (ideal)   _____

8.   coff   (beverage)   _____

9.   mmbr   (part of group)   _____

10. gntl   (kind)   _____

11. ntr   (come in)   _____

12. prtnd   (fake)   _____

LIVELY LANGUAGE ARTS

5
minutes

BLANKITY BLANKS

Activity
6

Directions

In ten minutes, how many words can you make by filling in the letter blanks below? Try to make 20.

C ____ ____ ____ E

_____   _____

_____   _____

_____   _____

_____   _____

_____   _____

_____   _____

_____   _____

_____   _____

_____   _____

10
minutes

FUNNY VERBS

Directions

Complete each joke by writing the appropriate verb from the box.

setting	sit	raise	rise	lay	lying
sat	sitting	raised	rising	lays	lie

LIVELY LANGUAGE ARTS

1. What's the best way to _____ guinea pigs?

   . . . Pick them up.

2. Why does the Statue of Liberty stand in the New York Harbor?

   . . . because it can't _____ down

3. When the banana couldn't sleep, why did it _____ still without making a sound?

   . . . It didn't want to wake the rest of the bunch.

4. Boy: "Why are you _____ on that clock?"

   Girl: "I want to be on time."

5. If a rooster _____ an egg at the peak of a slanted roof, on which side will it always fall?

   . . . neither side, because roosters don't _____ eggs!

6. What's dangerous about the sun _____ and the sun _____ ?

   . . . At these times, the day breaks and the night falls.

7. Why did your sister eat yeast and floor wax for breakfast?

   . . . because she wanted to _____ and shine

8. Why should you never believe what a person in a bed says?

   . . . because the person is _____

9. Patient: "Doc, I feel like I'm on pins and needles."

   Doctor: "Oops! You must have _____ on my knitting."

10. Two men went hunting. The first hunter _____ his rifle to shoot a goose.

    Friend: "Wait! That rifle isn't loaded."

    First hunter: "But the bird will be gone if I take the time to load!"

10 minutes

MISSING VOWELS

Activity

8

Directions

The following occupations have had their vowels removed.
Write the words correctly.

1. chmst _____

2. srvyr _____

3. bldr _____

4. rchtct _____

5. wtchmkr _____

6. brcklyr _____

7. tchr _____

8. jwlr _____

9. crpntr _____

10. plmbr _____

11. frmr _____

12. dntst _____

13. drvng nstrctr _____

14. lwyr _____

15. hrdrssr _____

16. scrtry _____

10 minutes

SWAP SHOPS

Directions

A shop owner asks her workers to stand in the street and advertise what her shop sells. Every time they stand together they advertise the wrong items. In each time, one person is standing in the wrong place. What does the shop really sell?

1. _____

2. _____

3. _____

LIVELY LANGUAGE ARTS

5 minutes

SYNONYMS

Activity
10

Directions

In the word search, find a synonym for each of the following groups of words below. Use the words in the box to help you.

```
T  I  K  F  H  A  O  L  E  R  E  D  C  D  X  S  O  A
Z  T  Z  R  G  K  Z  B  C  N  E  X  N  A  R  L  E  U
P  U  V  R  A  T  D  Y  O  J  L  M  C  I  T  D  P  S
Y  C  E  T  G  D  Q  D  L  R  V  E  C  I  H  C  F  C
W  E  Y  D  G  Y  D  I  F  F  I  C  U  L  T  E  H  B
D  U  L  G  W  N  Y  X  R  B  W  P  I  F  F  I  B  E
T  S  E  B  E  D  G  E  E  R  L  W  Z  P  A  N  N  B
B  L  L  P  Q  H  J  N  R  B  I  Q  V  E  Y  S  C  G
P  B  E  K  C  L  I  S  Y  A  W  L  A  E  V  L  T  J
W  J  O  S  J  M  G  W  I  D  L  L  C  D  O  L  L  T
X  Z  J  L  R  Y  D  I  N  E  H  U  P  S  W  V  C  G
Y  I  H  E  O  C  E  K  V  Z  N  F  E  E  R  E  N  S
X  G  T  S  H  L  U  A  V  L  E  I  H  O  P  L  D  X
W  E  C  R  Z  E  Q  C  D  U  K  T  D  X  H  G  H  E
D  P  K  D  Z  A  H  T  F  H  O  U  E  H  M  M  Y  Y
X  G  D  L  N  N  M  I  M  L  R  A  M  S  F  X  J  P
K  F  H  O  L  O  W  O  A  Y  B  E  L  O  W  W  W  Q
P  M  K  Z  P  N  N  N  I  Z  I  B  M  R  O  C  Y  C
```

action	beautiful	best	clean	deep	done	expect
agreed	behind	broken	close	determine	edge	fast
always	below	catch	dark	difficult	exciting	

1. tidy, neat, orderly
2. greatest, finest, paramount
3. decided, settled, arranged
4. quick, speedy, rapid
5. grasp, grip, clench
6. gorgeous, stunning, striking
7. thrilling, exhilarating, stirring
8. after, following, last
9. ready, complete, prepared
10. under, beneath, lower

11. wrecked, busted, kaput
12. lock, seal, secure
13. deed, feat, acomplishment
14. shady, shadowy, gloomy
15. profound, mysterious, meaningful
16. continually, constantly, permanently
17. decide, resolve, establish
18. rim, border, perimeter
19. complex, tricky, complicated
20. anticipate, suppose, presume

15
minutes

ANTONYMS

Activity
11

Directions

Fill in the crossword puzzle with the antonyms of the words below. Use the words in the box to help you. Clue #10 down has been done for you.

gain	guess
gave	guilty
general	hairy
get	handy
gift	happy
glance	harm
go	heard
great	heavy
grief	here
grow	hit

Across

The antonym of . . .

1. shrink
2. stay
3. give
5. specific
7. heal
8. lose
10. light
11. sad
12. there
13. joy
14. terrible

Down

The antonym of . . .

1. curse
2. took
3. know
4. stare
5. innocent
6. useless
9. bald
10. unheard
12. miss

10
minutes

14

LIVELY LANGUAGE ARTS

HELPING VERBS

Directions

Find the helping and the action verbs in the sentences below.

Helping Verbs									
am	is	has	are	were	was	have	had	can	will

1. An elephant is raising his trunk.

   helping: _____   action: _____

2. Amy has learned to bake pies.

   helping: _____   action: _____

3. Harold is drawing with a purple crayon.

   helping: _____   action: _____

4. We will drink the water.

   helping: _____   action: _____

5. She has taken the test before.

   helping: _____   action: _____

6. I have seen the bear.

   helping: _____   action: _____

7. We are going to the store.

   helping: _____   action: _____

8. Jenny can ride a bike.

   helping: _____   action: _____

9. I will eat all the cinnamon rolls.

   helping: _____   action: _____

LIVELY LANGUAGE ARTS

5 minutes

SPELL WELL

Activity
13

Directions

Many of the words below are spelled wrong. Find and color those that are spelled right.

brocolli	neice	margerine	anchor
envelope	assistant	portible	fourwards
accident	general	swiming	already
plumer	leopard	libary	beautifull
evry	separate	frown	platipus
usually	rythm	soldier	allways
answer	lizard	easily	truely
robust	cemetary	addmission	acomodation
theif	danger	careful	friend
minite	benefit	tomorrow	schedule

LIVELY LANGUAGE ARTS

10 minutes

16

FRONTS AND BACKS

Activity 14

Directions

The letters in the chart are the "fronts" and "backs" of words. See how many words you can make using the "fronts" and "backs" provided.

Fronts	Backs
re	sting
assi	ise
coa	gn
ru	sts
tru	ch
li	ts
disgu	uther
cru	ck
boa	mpet
prom	th

LIVELY LANGUAGE ARTS

_____

_____

_____

_____

_____

_____

_____   _____

_____   _____

_____   _____

_____   _____

_____   _____

_____   _____

_____   _____

5 minutes

MISSING CREATURES

Activity
15

Directions

Can you name the creatures whose names end with these words? The first one has been done for you.

1. _____pie   magpie _____

2. _____rich   _____

3. _____key   _____

4. _____rot   _____

5. _____pine   _____

6. _____at   _____

7. _____out   _____

8. _____use   _____

9. _____can   _____

10. _____fly   _____

LIVELY LANGUAGE ARTS

5 minutes

PARTS OF SPEECH

Directions

Categorize the words in the box into six categories. Place each word under the correct part of speech. Four words belong under each category.

eating	envelope	we	read
she	sleep	pretty	softly
thin	red	so	apron
happily	joyfully	and	but
it	jumped	Betsy Ross	yet
twenty	they	furiously	father

Nouns   **Verbs**   **Pronouns**

_____   _____   _____

_____   _____   _____

_____   _____   _____

_____   _____   _____

Conjunctions   **Adverbs**   **Adjectives**

_____   _____   _____

_____   _____   _____

_____   _____   _____

_____   _____   _____

Write a sentence using one word from each category. _____

10 minutes

_____

SMALL WORDS

Activity 17

Directions

Each small word in the box can be used to complete one of the words below. Write the small word in the correct space.

ill	last	rag	act	ear	in	name	chest

1. f_____ile → (easily broken)

2. f_____ory → (place where goods are made)

3. dr_____y → (dull, boring)

4. p_____k → (color)

5. m_____ion → (large number)

6. e_____ic → (stretchy material)

7. or_____ra → (group of musicians)

8. e_____l → (coating on teeth)

LIVELY LANGUAGE ARTS

5 minutes

ARITHMETIC

Activity
18

Directions

All the words fitting the clues below can be made from the letters of the word *arithmetic*. What are the words?

A R I T H M E T I C

1. seconds, minutes, hours   _____

2. a female horse   _____

3. you sit on it   _____

4. not wild   _____

5. a group of athletes   _____

6. the organ that pumps blood   _____

7. the fat of milk   _____

8. small rodent   _____

9. drop of liquid from the eye   _____

10. a school subject   _____

11. food from animals   _____

12. provides warmth   _____

LIVELY LANGUAGE ARTS

5
minutes

NAME _____ DATE _____

MIXED-UP MEALS

Activity
19

Directions

Tommy's brothers wanted to play a trick on him. They tore his shopping list in half and rearranged the letters on the second half. Match the beginnings and endings so Tommy knows what to buy. Then write his list in alphabetical order.

saus	ee
must	cuits
marg	ages
coff	ese
st	auce
ch	ard
bis	anas
s	arine
che	icken
ban	eak

Alphabetical Order

1. _____   6. _____

2. _____   7. _____

3. _____   8. _____

4. _____   9. _____

5. _____   10. _____

LIVELY LANGUAGE ARTS

10
minutes

Mix 'N Match

Activity
20

Directions

Find the first half of the word that matches the second half to make ten words that fit the clues.

1st Half	2nd Half
wal	nip
twe	hon
tur	ble
sta	ond
pyt	let
ham	ana
mar	ert
des	lve
ban	ble
alm	per

Clues   **Answers**

1. vegetable   _____

2. large snake   _____

3. type of nut   _____

4. holds paper money _____

5. holds dirty clothes _____

6. dry, barren land   _____

7. number   _____

8. hard rock   _____

9. home of a horse   _____

10. fruit   _____

10 minutes

LIVELY LANGUAGE ARTS

MULTIPLE MEANINGS

Activity 21

Directions

Select the word from the box that can be used to complete both sentences.

buckle	guard	pinch	plug	school	squash	touched	wax

1. The candle is made from _____.

   _____ the furniture before you set the table.

2. The _____ marches back and forth in front of the palace.

   The police officers will _____ the priceless treasure.

3. Do you like _____?

   Go _____ that giant pillow!

4. Don't forget to _____ your seatbelt.

   I won this belt _____ at the rodeo.

5. The _____ on the lamp was bent.

   Do not _____ up the sink with the vegetables.

6. The _____ of fish was swimming in the clear, blue water.

   Beverly goes to _____ every day.

7. She felt the _____ as the drawer closed on her fingers.

   The crab will _____ with its front claws.

8. The baby _____ her nose with her toes.

   I was _____ by his generosity.

5 minutes

24

LIVELY LANGUAGE ARTS

GIVE ME A "C"

Activity
22

Directions

Which of these imaginary guide word pairs would each word belong under in a dictionary? Write the words under the correct pair.

category	canopy	ceiling	century
caramel	celebrate	calves	candy
cave	candle	cereal	capable
centimeter	celery	ceremony	camel

call/cane

_____

_____

_____

_____

canine/cattle

_____

_____

_____

_____

caution/cement

_____

_____

_____

center/certain

_____

_____

_____

LIVELY LANGUAGE ARTS

10 minutes

HOMOPHONES

Activity
23

Directions

Select the correct homophone from the parentheses to fill in the blanks in the sentences below.

1. Washington, D.C., is the _____ of the United States. *(capital/capitol)*

2. To watch his sister Jane lose the race was more than John could _____. *(bear/bare)*

3. How many times have you _____ the doughnut shop without stopping? *(passed/past)*

4. Mother said, "Go to bed because _____ too late for you to be up on a school night." *(its/it's)*

5. "_____ going to clean up this mess?" my father asked about the spilled milk. *(Who's/Whose)*

6. The drum major _____ the band in the parade. *(lead/led)*

7. Do you think that the world will ever be completely at _____? *(peace/piece)*

8. The Wilson twins learned how to button _____ *(their/there/they're)* shirts when they were only _____ years old. *(to/too/two)*

9. I do not think it is _____ that my brother would not loan me bus _____. *(fair/fare)*

10. My editor does not think it is _____ that the judge will not allow me to _____ a newspaper story about the mysterious _____ that the barbarians were participating in. *(right/rite/write)*

11. Most young doctors learn to show _____ with all of their _____. *(patience/patients)*

12. I hope that our new _____ chef does not _____ us before the big banquet next week. *(desert/dessert)*

10 minutes

COMPOUND WORDS

Activity
24

Directions

Read the phrases that will give clues to two words. Join the words together to create a compound word. The first one has been done for you.

1. ____campground____ a place you go for a week in the summer + the floor you walk on

2. _____ used to cook with on a stove + put birthday candles into this

3. _____ to see + the opposite of in

4. _____ "a man's best friend" + your home

5. _____ a fairy pays you money for this + used to stick thinks together

6. _____ found on the beaches + made of cardboard

7. _____ great or wonderful + another word for mom

8. _____ opposite of under + flat wood for building

9. _____ a woman + a crawling insect

10. _____ opposes your finger + to pin something up

11. _____ at the end of your arm + wiggle and jiggle

12. _____ petals are on this + boil water in this

13. _____ you shake with this + paper or plastic

14. _____ your fifth "finger" + not cursive but . . .

15. _____ in a sandbox + comes with thunder and lightning

16. _____ goes oink + used to keep sheep inside

17. _____ you sleep on it + what a clock tells

LIVELY LANGUAGE ARTS

10 minutes

WHICH WORD?

Activity
25

Directions

Words that sound or look alike often have meanings that are not alike at all. Decide which word of the two choices on the right is the correct one to correspond with the word or phrase on the left, and then color in that box.

LIVELY LANGUAGE ARTS

1. dry land	desert / dessert
2. Carson City, Nevada	capital / capitol
3. complete	through / thorough
4. in any case	any way / anyway
5. a result	affect / effect
6. to hint or suggest	imply / infer
7. second in a series of two	later / latter
8. a heavenly body	angel / angle
9. unlawful	illicit / elicit
10. to prove something is false	disapprove / disprove
11. writing paper	stationary / stationery
12. to take that which is offered	accept / except
13. to go forward	precede / proceed
14. a part of speech	preposition / proposition
15. to stop	quit / quite

5 minutes

FIXING ERRORS

Activity
26

Directions

Rewrite the following sentences, correcting any errors you find.

1. I dont want no nasty pigeons roosting on my ford pickup, said my Father.

_____

_____

2. We are camping in the dessert fore the memorial day weekend, and going hikeing.

_____

_____

3. Rosa bought peeches grapes and apricots when she went to the Supermarket.

_____

_____

4. My favrite pies are maid with rhubarb and gooseberrys they are sweet and sour.

_____

_____

5. My mother was bourne on febuary 14 1970 in new Orleans Luisiana.

_____

_____

6. My father is from the state of Main and he is stationed in portland with the U.S. coast guard.

_____

_____

7. Using a word processer, can be helpfull for both the begininng and the experenced writer.

_____

_____

8. Marias van dyed twice on the Freeway and she decided to by a knew car.

_____

_____

LIVELY LANGUAGE ARTS

10 minutes

TRANSITIONS

Directions

Choose one transition from the box to connect each of the following pairs of sentences. Use each transition word only once.

afterwards	otherwise	for example	however
meanwhile	on the other hand	furthermore	in fact
as a result	finally	therefore	next
consequently	moreover	for instance	

Example: The sidewalk ended; nevertheless, we walked on in the rain.

1. Undri is always late. He was 30 minutes late to class yesterday.

_____

_____

2. Mr. Yates introduced the speaker. He sat down.

_____

_____

3. The construction crew could not get the materials. They could not finish the job.

_____

_____

4. Tory became tired of doing her sister's work. She had her own work to do.

_____

_____

5. Welton did not dislike the movie. He enjoyed it immensely.

_____

_____

6. Zenia missed the first bus. She arrived on time.

_____

_____

7. Vladimir always follows instructions. He makes good grades.

_____

_____

15 minutes

FIGURATIVE LANGUAGE

Directions

Create both a simile and a metaphor to describe each of the following events. An example has been done for you.

Example: your brother pole vaulting

Simile: My brother launches himself like a rocket when he pole vaults.

Metaphor: My brother is a soaring rocket when he pole vaults.

1. a balloon floating up into the sky

Simile:_____

Metaphor: _____

2. a monkey eating a banana

Simile:_____

Metaphor: _____

3. a five-year-old child learning to ice skate

Simile:_____

Metaphor: _____

4. a goose flying south for the winter

Simile:_____

Metaphor: _____

5. a baby bird learning to fly

Simile:_____

Metaphor: _____

LIVELY LANGUAGE ARTS

15 minutes

SEQUENCE

Activity 29

Directions

Read the story, and then number the events in the order in which they occurred.

B-Ball

Eddie has always been into sports. Before playing basketball, he played soccer. His soccer team went to the state championships and won a trophy when he was in the fifth grade. It was a very exciting game, and Eddie scored the winning goal!

Now Eddie plays basketball on the ninth-grade basketball team. Next year, he will try out for the tenth-grade soccer team, as well. Then he will be playing team sports practically all year round. When Eddie was five years old, his big sister took him to a college soccer game, and that's when he decided that he wanted to play on a sports team.

Today, his sister Jessica comes to his basketball games and claims that she inspired him to be the great athlete that he is. Eddie just laughs when she says that, but he does agree that she had a part in his love for athletics. Jessica frequently tells him that if he works hard he can do anything. Eddie's most recent dream is to go to college on a basketball scholarship and study physics.

_____ Eddie plays on the ninth-grade basketball team.

_____ Eddie decides that he wants to play on a sports team.

_____ Eddie's fifth-grade soccer team won the state championships.

_____ Eddie hopes to go to college and study physics.

_____ Eddie scored the winning goal on his fifth-grade soccer team.

_____ Eddie will try out for the tenth-grade soccer team.

LIVELY LANGUAGE ARTS

10 minutes

BIG IDEAS

Activity 30

Directions

In the box below, you will find 10 ideas or topics. There are 10 lists below that need a main idea. Take the ideas from the box and write them at the top of the lists below.

| Favorite Foods | Favorite Rides | Sports | Pet Peeves | Travel |
| Homework | School | Summer | Ice Cream | Chores |

1. _____

Dust makes me sneeze.

Takes too much time.

Boring

2. _____

Pizza

Candy

Burritos

3. _____

Recess

Study Hall

Library

4. _____

People who cut in line

Losing my lunch money

Alarm clocks

5. _____

Creamy, cold, and sweet

Banana splits

Hot fudge sundaes

6. _____

Books

Assignment schedule

Where to work at home

7. _____

Roller coasters

Loop rides

Spinning rides

8. _____

Packing

Tickets and reservations

Souvenirs

9. _____

Swimming

Ice Cream

Vacations

10. _____

Basketball

Hockey

Baseball

LIVELY LANGUAGE ARTS

5 minutes

A Pretend Election

Activity **31**

Directions

Read the following news story about an election. Use the mini dictionary to help you fill in the missing words. Then in the box below, draw a line to match each idea with the best new word.

---

veep — abbreviation of "vice-president"

dictator — a leader with complete power

predict — to guess, usually based on studying information

declare — to say

reform — to improve by removing problems

biannual — twice a year

Election Blog

In the next few days, we expect Reginald Mifflestaff to once again (**1.**) _____ that he is running for president of our science club for the 8th time. Since our elections are (**2.**) _____ , that means he has been in power for 4 years. It's easy to (**3.**) _____ who will win the election, because, just like with the last seven, Mifflestaff will be the only person running! Everyone knows that that he is a (**4.**) _____ and not a president. This can be seen even in many things that he says, such as his answer as to why he doesn't have a vice-president. "I don't need a (**5.**) _____ ," he said. "I can do it all myself." Somebody else needs to step forward and take charge of this organization. Our club needs (**6.**) _____ , and it starts at the top!

---

7. "We'll do this every six months."		**A.** veep
8. "I'm the boss! You do what I tell you to do."		**B.** dictator
9. "Let's change how we do things."		**C.** predict
10. "I think the Colts will win next year's Super Bowl."		**D.** declare
11. "I am second in command."		**E.** reform
12. "I am one of the best dressers in the 5th grade."		**F.** biannual

10 minutes

LIVELY LANGUAGE ARTS

DANCE FEVER

Activity 32

Directions

Read the story, and then answer the questions that follow.

Dance Fever was a group of neighborhood girls who loved to dance and put on performances. The girls practiced for hours on end. Finally, the day of the show arrived.

All the girls were afraid they would forget their parts. But that wasn't the problem at all. In fact, they were about to face their worst fear ever.

Lights, camera, action! It was time for the show. The girls put on their costumes and got ready backstage. The parents were assembling in the audience section of the basement. There was a slight glitch in the technical equipment, but that was soon **remedied**.

The first two dances went off without a hitch. The next dance required a pyramid by the girls. They had practiced this part over and over. The problem came when Ashlyn slipped on Lexi's knee. It was an innocent mistake that had drastic results. Ashlyn came tumbling down. Along with her went Lexi, Caitlyn, Anne, and Elise. It was a pile of arms and legs. Moans and groans were heard from the girls. A gasp rose from the audience.

With nothing left to do, the girls all rose to their feet and took a bow. This thrilled the audience, who were afraid of what might happen next. The audience jumped to their feet, giving the girls a standing ovation. In a most unexpected way, the girls had gotten the response they had dreamed of!

LIVELY LANGUAGE ARTS

1. Which paragraph explains the problem in the story?
   a. first paragraph
   b. last paragraph
   c. third paragraph
   d. fourth paragraph

2. What inferences can you make about the Dance Fever girls?
   a. They are strict with each other.
   b. They have very high expectations.
   c. They don't take themselves too seriously and can adjust easily.
   d. They are learning about peer pressure.

3. What is the meaning of the word *remedied* as used in the story?
   a. resolved
   b. quickly
   c. instrumental
   d. systematically

10 minutes

An Unusual Inmate

LIVELY LANGUAGE ARTS

Directions

Read the passage, and then answer the questions that follow.

In 1924, Pep, a black Labrador retriever, lived in Pennsylvania. Then one day he killed the governor's cat. The governor **ardently** loved his cat. He was so furious that he demanded that Pep go to jail. People thought that he wasn't serious. So the governor put on his judge's robes. He had Pep brought into court. However, there was no jury at Pep's trial. The judge simply pronounced the sentence: "Life imprisonment without the possibility of parole."

Pep went to prison, but he never lived in a cell. Instead he went wherever he pleased within the prison walls. He had a good life because so many of the inmates loved him. He followed them around while they did their assigned chores. Pep was petted and played with until he died in a fellow prisoner's arms in 1930.

1. Why did Pep have to go to jail?
   a. His owner didn't want him anymore.
   b. The other inmates needed company.
   c. He had killed the governor's cat.

2. Why did the judge say Pep could never be paroled?
   a. The judge wanted Pep to confess to the crime.
   b. The judge didn't want Pep to ever leave the prison.
   c. The judge wanted the jury's support for his decision.

3. Why did the author choose the title?
   a. Pep acted strangely for a dog.
   b. Dogs are rarely put in jail.
   c. The other inmates loved Pep very much.

4. The word *ardently* means . . .
   a. wrongly.
   b. mildly.
   c. strongly.

10 minutes

LLAMAS

Directions

Read the passage, and then answer the questions that follow.

Do you know what a llama is? Do you know how to say that word? A llama is an interesting animal. In English, the word is pronounced with the 'l' sound at the beginning (*lama*). In Spanish, the word is pronounced with a 'y' sound at the beginning (*yama*). The llama comes from South America. Llamas have been used as pack animals for thousands of years. They are strong and smart animals. They can hike on the toughest trails. The llama is able to carry over 200 pounds and can hike about 12 hours in a day. They are similar to camels and cows, in that they chew their own cud.

A llama can grow to be as big as 400 pounds. The life span of a llama is 15 to 29 years. Llamas come in a variety of colors. They can be brown, gray, black, or white, as well as a combination of colors. Llamas are herd animals and prefer to be with other llamas. Llamas are also known for spitting. They typically spit to show **dominance** to other llamas. They can see very well, and sometimes they are used to protect baby cows, sheep, or goats.

Llamas do make some noises. They can be heard humming, which sounds a lot like how you sound humming. They may also cluck or make an alarm sound. They use the alarm sound when they feel threatened or afraid. Llamas are also known to roll on the ground to fluff their wool. They prefer to roll in the dirt.

1. What is this passage mainly about?
   a. how the llama eats
   b. predators of the llama
   c. the different types of llama
   d. general facts about the llama

2. In the second paragraph, what does the word *dominance* mean?
   a. supremacy
   b. broken
   c. structured
   d. overcome

3. Llamas are social animals and prefer to . . .
   a. hunt other animals.
   b. protect other animals.
   c. live in groups.
   d. roll on their backs.

4. Based on information in the passage, why are llamas good pack animals?
   a. They stay in groups.
   b. They are black and white.
   c. They are smaller than camels.
   d. They can carry a lot of weight.

10
minutes

TALL TALES

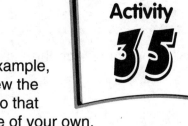

Activity 35

Directions

When people tell "tall tales" they exaggerate. For example, a line from a tall tale could be, "It was so windy it blew the dogs off their chains!" Finish the sentences below so that they could be part of a tall tale. Then make up some of your own.

1. It was so cloudy that _____

_____

2. The dogs were barking so loudly _____

_____

3. People were running _____

_____

4. The children were so scared _____

_____

5. _____

_____

6. _____

_____

_____

7. _____

_____

LIVELY LANGUAGE ARTS

10 minutes

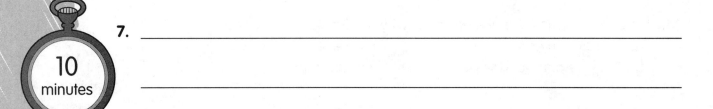

SQUARE PATHWAYS

Activity 36

Directions

Color all the squares red counting by 7s to 140.
Color all the squares blue counting by 8s to 144.

7s path ↓   **8s path** ↓

15	7	12	8	16	8	80	74	91
14	4	11	12	24	41	91	83	86
21	16	14	18	32	40	37	107	48
28	35	42	17	61	48	61	53	17
11	17	49	33	38	56	112	119	36
63	56	91	72	64	105	36	144	126
70	18	43	80	98	44	136	128	133
15	77	84	91	88	96	104	120	140
47	86	93	57	60	108	116	112	133

5 minutes

Tricky Triangles

Activity
37

Directions

How many triangles can you find in this diagram?

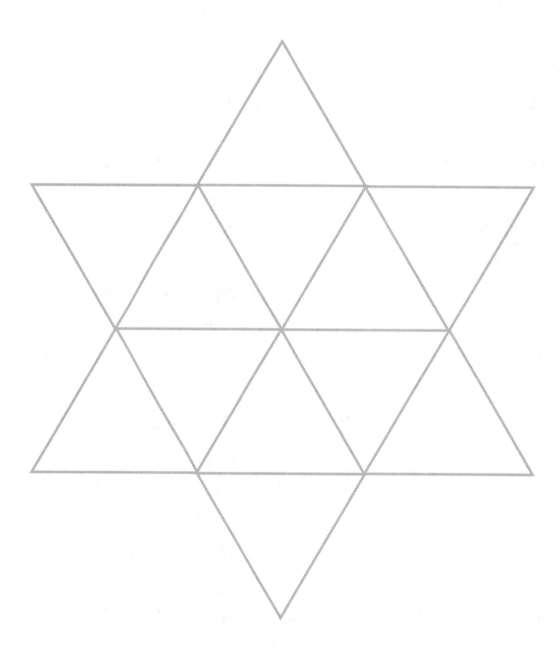

MIND-BENDER MATH

5
minutes

There are _____ triangles.

SALE TIME

Directions

A supermarket had a sale in which the goods were priced according to the letters in their names. How much did each of the following cost?

> **50¢ for each vowel**
>
> **15¢ for each consonant**

1. flour _____

2. bread _____

3. margarine _____

4. peaches _____

5. sausages _____

6. peanut butter _____

7. string cheese _____

8. whole milk _____

9. pasta sauce _____

10. salad dressing _____

MIND-BENDER MATH

15 minutes

SYMMETRY

Directions

Complete the other side of these pictures so they are symmetrical.

MIND-BENDER MATH

1.

2.

3.

5 minutes

MATH TERMS A TO Z

Activity
40

Directions

Find each math term below in the word search.

```
R   O   G   C   V   O   L   U   M   E   A   J   Y   K
T   A   U   R   E   H   T   D   I   W   W   W   A   I
A   D   E   N   I   N   F   I   N   I   T   E   R   L
B   S   N   N   C   D   T   T   A   G   G   N   D   O
L   O   E   E   I   E   V   I   T   E   O   P   H   G
E   L   T   I   D   L   S   C   M   I   R   O   V   R
Q   U   A   D   R   I   L   A   T   E   R   A   L   A
L   T   M   E   Z   X   V   C   C   I   T   J   U   M
A   I   I   S   D   S   N   I   Z   O   R   E   Z   T
R   O   T   A   M   U   R   O   D   G   Q   Q   R   S
E   N   S   B   F   T   N   N   I   O   J   V   N   I
M   R   E   R   E   T   E   M   I   R   E   P   B   X
U   A   U   M   A   R   H   O   M   B   U   S   E   A
N   U   V   L   N   W   O   N   K   N   U   F   H   X
```

AREA	JOIN	SOLUTION
BASE	KILOGRAM	TABLE
CENTIMETER	LINEAR	UNKNOWN
DIVIDEND	METRIC	VOLUME
ESTIMATE	NUMERAL	WIDTH
FUNCTION	OUNCE	X-AXIS
GRID	PERIMETER	YARD
HORIZONTAL	QUADRILATERAL	ZERO
INFINITE	RHOMBUS	

MIND-BENDER MATH

10 minutes

CIRCLING AROUND

Activity
41

Directions

In each circle, the center number is the total of some of the numbers around the circle. Color these numbers.

MIND-BENDER MATH

1.
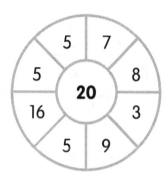

5.
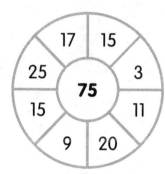

2.
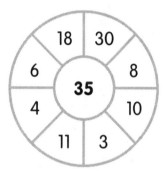

6.
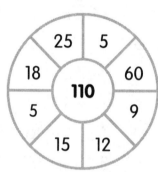

3.
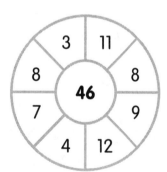

7.
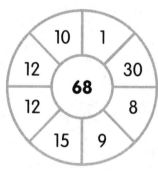

4.
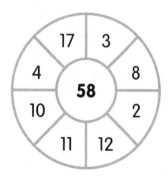

8.
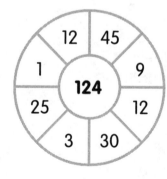

15 minutes

COMMON SIDES

Activity 42

Directions

Color in all the pairs of triangles that share a common side and add up to 21.

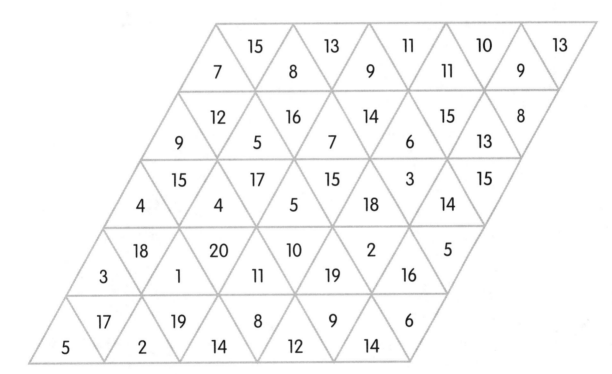

What sign do the colored triangles make? _____

5 minutes

MAGIC SQUARES

Activity
43

Directions

Write in the missing numbers to complete each square.
The three numbers in any line (across, down, or diagonally)
must add up to the number in the circle.

1.

(9)

		4
2		1

4.

(21)

5		
11	1	

2.

(18)

	7	
9	5	

5.

(15)

1		
6	7	

3.

(12)

7		1
		5

6.

(30)

	15	6
14		

10 minutes

TOTALS

Activity
44

Directions

Look at the numbers in the shapes, and then answer the questions that follow.

```
        6
    4       3          7        3    2
    4       2     9    5        4    7
    4            5  6  8
                6
               3    4  5
          4    6    5
```

1. What is the total of the numbers in the circle, but not in any other shape?

_____

2. What is the total of the numbers in both the triangle and the circle, but not in any other shape?

_____

3. What is the total of the numbers in the rectangle, but not in any other shape?

_____

4. What is the total of all the numbers not in the rectangle?

_____

5
minutes

MIND-BENDER MATH

NUMBER ROWS

Activity
45

Directions

Use the numbers in the grid to answer the questions that follow.

MIND-BENDER MATH

A	4	6	12	10	11	15	3
B	18	23	7	19	24	6	8
C	11	13	27	7	9	15	19
D	60	48	32	90	24	18	12
E	3	9	16	18	4	0	15
F	17	8	4	9	3	2	17

1. Which row consists of all odd numbers?   _____

2. Which row contains only even numbers?   _____

3. Which row contains the most odd numbers under 20?   _____

4. Which row has the same number listed twice?   _____

5. In which row do all the numbers add up to 105?   _____

10
minutes

TOUCHY NUMBERS

Activity
46

Directions

Fill in the blank boxes with the numbers 1–5. Each full row and column contains the numbers 1, 2, 3, 4, and 5. Each shaded number is the sum of all the numbers touching it.

1.

4	1	5		
	26		**23**	3
		4	2	1
5	**25**	2	**23**	4
2	3	1	4	

3.

5		2	3	1
3	**25**	1	**21**	5
			3	
	25		**27**	3
			3	4

2.

4	1			5
2	**22**	1	**20**	3
		2	3	
1	**28**		**22**	4
3		5	1	2

4.

2		4		
	20	1	**25**	
		2		4
	26	3	**24**	
	4		2	1

MIND-BENDER MATH

20 minutes

FINDING COORDINATES

Activity 47

Directions

Use the points on the coordinate grid to answer the riddle at the bottom of the page. Write the letter at each location on the lines.

MIND-BENDER MATH

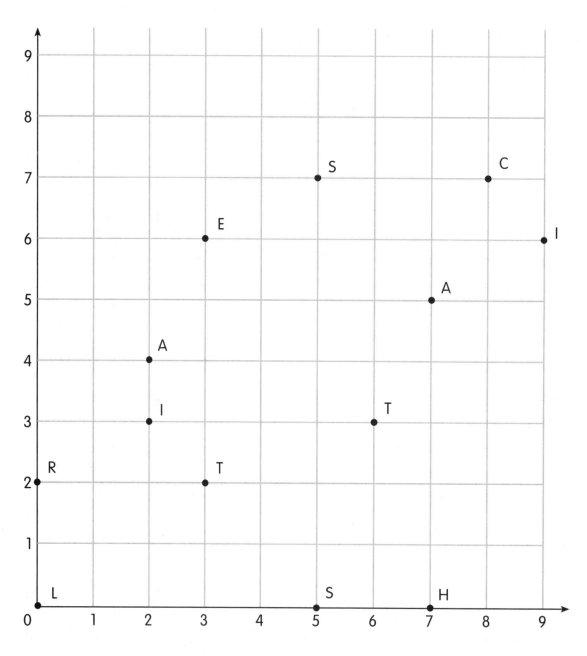

5 minutes

How do you make a hot dog stand?

$\overline{\text{(5,7)}}$ $\overline{\text{(6,3)}}$ $\overline{\text{(3,6)}}$ $\overline{\text{(7,5)}}$ $\overline{\text{(0,0)}}$　　$\overline{\text{(2,3)}}$ $\overline{\text{(3,2)}}$ $\overline{\text{(5,0)}}$　　$\overline{\text{(8,7)}}$ $\overline{\text{(7,0)}}$ $\overline{\text{(2,4)}}$ $\overline{\text{(9,6)}}$ $\overline{\text{(0,2)}}$

NUMBER QUIZ

Activity
48

Directions

Study the series of numbers, and then answer the questions that follow.

a. 2,546
b. 6,804
c. 8,950
d. 5,678
e. 1,654
f. 10,674
g. 4,821

MIND-BENDER MATH

1. Which is the largest of the numbers? _____

2. Which is the smallest of the numbers? _____

3. If you added the digits, what number would add up to 26? _____

4. If you multiplied all the digits, what number would equal 240? _____

5. Which number is not divisible by 2? _____

6. Which number is divisible by both 10 and 5? _____

7. What is the difference between the largest and the smallest number? _____

8. What is the total if you add numbers b, c, and d? _____

10
minutes

SUDOKU CHALLENGE

Activity 49

Directions

Each row, column, and 3 x 3 box has the digits 1, 2, 3, 4, 5, 6, 7, 8, and 9. Fill in the blanks to complete the puzzles. How many can you complete in 20 minutes?

MIND-BENDER MATH

1.

5		6		2	8	3		
	4		6			5	2	
8		9			7		4	6
		7		6	5	2	1	
		4				6		
	6	1	7	4		9		
6	7		1			4		2
	9	2			6		5	
		5	2	7		8		9

3.

		2	4				9	3
	7			2		6	8	
5	1		3	6		4		
	3	8		4	5	7		2
7								9
2		6	7	9		1	4	
		5	3	1			7	4
	2	7		8			1	
1	8				7	2		

2.

	1		2			9		
	9	8	6	4		1	3	
	6	2		9			5	8
		3	1	7		6		
2	4						1	9
	7		5	2	3			
4	3			1		9	2	
	2	1		6	9	5	7	
	5			3		4		

4.

7		4	8		5			3
9		2			3		6	8
	1			7		2	4	
8	7		2	9		6		
6								9
		9		3	6		8	2
	8	6	3				9	
4	3		6			8		7
2			1		4	3		6

20 minutes

THE VALUE OF WORDS

Activity
50

Directions

In the value box, each letter of the alphabet has been given a dollar value. To find the value of a word, add the values of all the letters. For example, the word "school" would be worth $72 (19 + 3 + 8 + 15 + 15 + 12 = 72). Write three words with appropriate values in each of the boxes below.

$10–$20 Words	$21–$50 Words

$51–$75 Words	$76–$100 Words

$101–$150 Words	$151–$200 Words

Value Box	
A	= $1
B	= $2
C	= $3
D	= $4
E	= $5
F	= $6
G	= $7
H	= $8
I	= $9
J	= $10
K	= $11
L	= $12
M	= $13
N	= $14
O	= $15
P	= $16
Q	= $17
R	= $18
S	= $19
T	= $20
U	= $21
V	= $22
W	= $23
X	= $24
Y	= $25
Z	= $26

MIND-BENDER MATH

20 minutes

NAME _____   DATE _____

ADDITION BOXES

Directions

Fill in the blanks using the digits 1–9 so that the sum of each row is the shaded number to the right, and the sum of each column is the shaded number below it. You can use a number more than once.

MIND-BENDER MATH

1.

2	9		7	**23**
3	6			**14**
			9	**20**
5	9		2	**23**

16	**27**	**15**	**22**

3.

	8	6		9	**28**
9	6			5	**26**
1	2		2	2	**9**
9		5	7		**32**
	5	2	8		**26**

29	**29**	**18**	**22**	**23**

2.

4		3		**25**
1	5		7	**17**
	2		3	**12**
3				**15**

10	**20**	**14**	**25**

4.

3		2	5	7	**21**
7	6	4			**22**
5	1		3		**17**
		6	8	3	**29**
	4	7		2	**23**

20	**24**	**25**	**25**	**18**

20 minutes

COIN COMBINATIONS

Directions

Figure out which coins are needed for each money combination below.
Write the number of each needed coin beside its picture.

1. Sondra Sorich opened her piggy bank so she could go to the mall. She found 11 coins worth $2.11. What coins did she have?

 _____   _____   _____   _____   _____

2. Bertha Biggspender found 13 coins worth $3.03 in her makeup bag. She did not have any dimes. Which coins did she find?

 _____   _____   _____   _____   _____

3. Maggie Moneytoes found 20 coins worth $3.27 in her shoe. She did not have any nickels. Which coins did she find?

 _____   _____   _____   _____   _____

4. Johnny Cashless kept his money in an old sock. He had 19 coins worth $4.51. He did not have a half dollar. Which coins did he have?

 _____   _____   _____   _____   _____

5. Mr. Monnebaggs had 14 coins worth $3.97 in his office safe. He did not have any dimes. Which coins did he have?

 _____   _____   _____   _____   _____

20 minutes

MISSING SIGNS

Activity 53

Directions

Fill in the missing math signs to make each number sentence true.

MIND-BENDER MATH

1. 3 ☐ 2 ☐ 4 = 10

2. 8 ☐ 8 ☐ 6 = 10

3. 20 ☐ 5 ☐ 4 = 8

4. 12 ☐ 4 ☐ 2 = 16

5. 14 ☐ 6 ☐ 10 = 30

6. 20 ☐ 4 ☐ 6 = 10

7. 5 ☐ 3 ☐ 5 = 20

8. 30 ☐ 6 ☐ 12 = 17

9. 40 ☐ 20 ☐ 20 = 0

10. 7 ☐ 7 ☐ 2 = 28

10 minutes

PICTURE PROBLEM

Activity
54

Directions

Solve the math problems in the grid, and then draw the pictures in the boxes below that contain the right answers. If you do it correctly, the second grid will make a picture of an animal.

7 x 6	3 x 5	10 x 9	7 x 4	100 ÷ 20	8 x 8
55 x 2	75 ÷ 3	2 x 18	8 x 4	40 – 19	10 + 7
96 ÷ 2	9 x 9	10 x 7	12 x 2	15 x 3	2 x 25
10 – 9	10 x 3	6 x 3	5 x 8	144 ÷ 12	10 x 6

40	25	36	5	1	24
12	18	60	21	17	15
90	110	45	30	48	50
70	28	32	42	81	64

10 minutes

GEOMETRICAL CHALLENGE

Directions

Each section of the figure below is labeled with a letter.
Your task is to find out which color and whole number goes
in each section. The possible colors are red, orange, yellow,
green, blue, and purple. Use the following clues to help you.
Write your answers in each section.

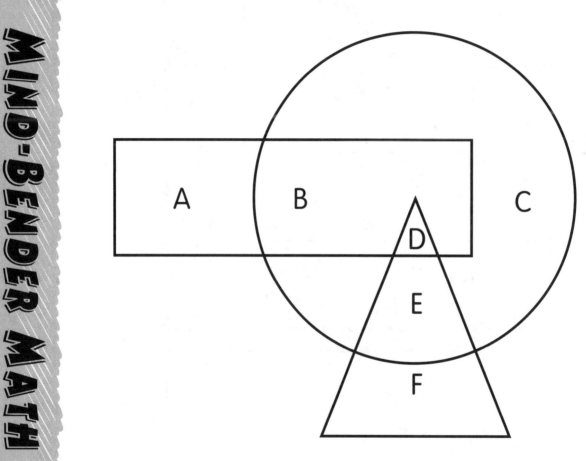

Clues:

- The sum of the triangle is 18.
- The region that is in all three shapes is colored green.
- The rectangle has the red, orange, and green regions in it.
- The yellow region is the number 8.
- The product of section D and the blue section is 30.

- The 5 section is green.
- A is red.
- The sum of the rectangle is 10.
- E is blue.
- The sum of the circle is 21.
- The sum of A and B is 5.
- The sum of C and F is 15.

15
minutes

NAME _____ DATE _____

WHAT'S THE END?

Directions

Start with the number given at the top of each table. Then follow through each step and write the answers in the column on the right.

1.

Start with 30	
double it	
subtract 10	
divide by 5	
add 40	
multiply by 6	

3.

Start with 12	
multiply by 4	
double it	
divide it by 4	
halve it	
triple it	

2.

Start with 70	
double it	
double it again	
add 500	
divide by 3	
multiply by 10	

4.

Start with 750	
double it	
divide it by 3	
subtract 250	
halve it	
divide by 5	

MIND-BENDER MATH

5
minutes

FOLLOW THE CLUES

Activity
57

Directions

Follow the clues to find the mystery numbers.

1,281,096	232,398	669,761	941,093
136,777	410,415	842,151	951,010
161,918	613,124	854,721	953,688
225,579	641,438	883,934	976,143

- Cross off the numbers that can be evenly divided by 3.
- Cross off the numbers that have the same number of odd and even digits.
- Cross off the numbers that are even.
- Cross off the number that has the greatest number of odd digits.

1. What is the mystery number? _____

- -

1,281,096	4,410,933	5,556,169	6,485,101
1,886,807	4,486,864	8,276,935	8,945,532
1,942,781	4,726,783	6,752,022	9,108,106
3,100,014	5,125,536	7,370,429	9,492,784

- Cross off the numbers that have two of the same digit in a row.
- Cross off the numbers that have three of the same digit in a row.
- Cross off the numbers that have the same digit used exactly twice in the number.

2. What is the mystery number? _____

20
minutes

MIND-BENDER MATH

FOUR SIGNS

Activity
58

Directions

Add the appropriate signs (+, −, x, ÷) to complete each problem. Each sign is used one time in each math problem. Solve each problem going from left to right.

1. 187   91 ☐ 8 ☐ 6 ☐ 3 = ___75___

2. 210 ☐ 4   105 ☐ 45 ☐ 30 = ___30___

3. 64 ☐ 4 ☐ 8 ☐ 105   110 = ___133___

4. 104   33 ☐ 61 ☐ 4 ☐ 8 = ___66___

5. 64 ☐ 77 ☐ 3   9 ☐ 99 = ___324___

6. 76 ☐ 4   84 ☐ 2 ☐ 194 = ___0___

7. 77 ☐ 12 ☐ 6 ☐ 10   31 = ___70___

8. 47 ☐ 109   83 ☐ 6 ☐ 6 = ___73___

20
minutes

         #2940 101 Activities for Fast Finishers

WHEEL OF FUN

Activity
59

Directions

Solve the division equations in the wheel of fun. Match the letters on the wheel with the answers below to crack the code.

MIND-BENDER MATH

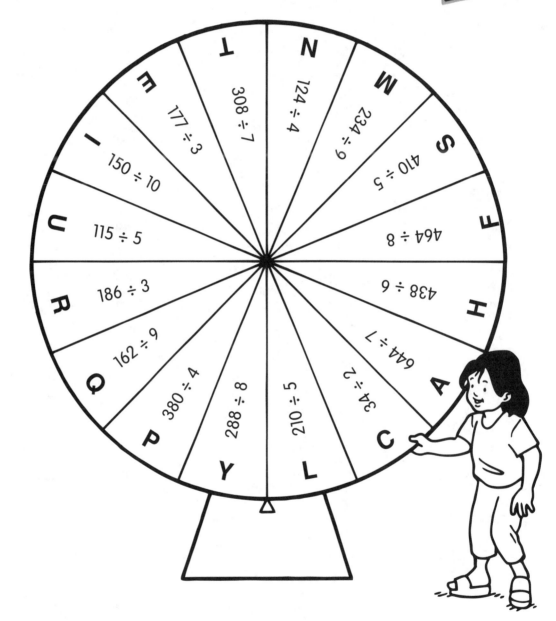

Wheel equations and letters:

- E — 150 ÷ 10
- T — 177 ÷ 3
- N — 124 ÷ 4
- M — 234 ÷ 9
- S — 410 ÷ 5
- F — 464 ÷ 8
- H — 438 ÷ 6
- A — 644 ÷ 7
- C — 34 ÷ 2
- L — 210 ÷ 5
- Y — 288 ÷ 8
- P — 380 ÷ 4
- Q — 162 ÷ 9
- R — 186 ÷ 3
- U — 115 ÷ 5
- I — 308 ÷ 7

15 minutes

___ ___ ___   ___ ___ ___ ___ ___ ___ ___
44 59 31   26 15 31 23 44 59 82

___ ___ ___ ___   ___ ___ ___ ___ !
58 62 59 59   95 42 92 36

NUMBER PUZZLE

Directions

Solve each math problem below. Write your answers in the number puzzle.

1.	**2.**	**3.**		**4.**	**5.**
6.					
	7.			**8.**	
9.					
		10.	**11.**		**12.**
13.			**14.**		

MIND-BENDER MATH

Across

1. 888 ÷ 2
4. 50 – 3
6. 1,304 + 1,304
7. 12 x 7
8. 9 x 7
9. 100 – 45
10. 2,000 + 500 + 40 + 4
13. 8 x 4
14. 660 – 1

Down

1. 7 x 6
2. 4,000 + 600 + 80 + 5
3. 2 x 202
5. 500 + 200 + 30 + 3
8. 7,000 – 755
9. 2 x 200 + 163
11. 8 x 7
12. 7 x 7

10 minutes

NAME _____   DATE _____

Answer Match

Activity
61

Directions

Look at the left and right sides in the columns below. On each side, there are equations that have the same answer. Draw lines between equations that have the same answer. The first one has been done for you.

834 ÷ 417	268 ÷ 67
117 ÷ 39	504 ÷ 8
224 ÷ 56	259 ÷ 37
225 ÷ 45	243 + 987
6 x 24	18 ÷ 6
17 x 32	8 x 68
13 x 28	402 ÷ 67
14 x 44	22 x 28
9 x 72	3 x 95
15 x 43	348 ÷ 174
534 ÷ 89	8 x 18
19 x 15	5 x 129
9 x 7	984 − 979
4 + 3	6 x 108
358 + 872	14 x 26

MIND-BENDER MATH

15 minutes

MULTIPLICATION MADNESS

Activity 62

Directions

Solve each multiplication problem. Write each product in the puzzle.

Across

1. 9,565 x 40 =

2. 5,937 x 87 =

5. 8,874 x 15 =

9. 1,655 x 88 =

10. 8,483 x 88 =

12. 7,774 x 29 =

14. 7,523 x 14 =

15. 1,020 x 29 =

16. 7,191 x 62 =

17. 9,727 x 77 =

18. 9,371 x 29 =

MIND-BENDER MATH

Down

1. 4,591 x 67 =

3. 2,516 x 54 =

4. 8,319 x 40 =

6. 7,194 x 19 =

7. 3,805 x 91 =

8. 4,936 x 56 =

11. 5,126 x 24 =

13. 7,264 x 84 =

16. 8,062 x 60 =

20 minutes

FRED THE FROG

Directions

Help Fred the frog reach his lily pad. He moves only vertically or horizontally—NOT diagonally! He can only hop onto numbers that are divisible by 7, 9, or 11. Color Fred's path from Start to Finish.

5,776	1,189	4,118	2,356	1,173	1,548	6,820	1,029	704	**Finish**
1,073	361	899	226	1,955	266	1,615	901	1,209	897
915	1,116	6,631	4,059	1,360	5,643	1,736	5,889	745	158
713	810	901	760	584	2,410	602	585	345	6,105
5,615	1,196	799	1,411	1,222	6,760	609	1,404	1,027	319
713	2,002	801	189	1,177	986	1,612	605	884	2,957
1,020	2,429	1,380	570	3,384	522	1,099	946	625	157
1,037	737	979	1,003	2,920	1,564	530	697	539	811
578	246	623	1,131	409	818	794	376	263	7,057
121	1,792	963	219	304	1,102	4,112	2,876	3,006	914

Start

15 minutes

MISSING INTEGERS

Activity **64**

Directions

Find the value of the missing integer (n) in each equation. Then write each answer as a number word in the puzzle. See #1 Across. It has been done for you.

Across

1. 2n = 4   n = __2__

4. 8n = 32   n = _____

5. 20 ÷ n = 2   n = _____

6. 2n = 6   n = _____

9. 27 ÷ n = 3   n = _____

11. 12 ÷ n = 6   n = _____

13. 9n = 63   n = _____

14. 5n = 30   n = _____

Down

1. 3n = 9   n = _____

2. 4 ÷ n = 4   n = _____

3. 16 ÷ n = 4   n = _____

4. 15 ÷ n = 3   n = _____

5. 8n = 16   n = _____

6. 30 ÷ n = 10   n = _____

7. 80 ÷ n = 10   n = _____

8. 2n = 12   n = _____

10. 10n = 50   n = _____

12. 8 ÷ n = 8   n = _____

13. 30 ÷ n = 5   n = _____

14. 10n = 70   n = _____

MIND-BENDER MATH

15 minutes

FRACTION FUN

Directions

Multiply the fractions, and use the letter for each answer to decode the hidden message at the bottom. Reduce answers to lowest terms.

Activity 65

1. (A) $\frac{8}{12} \times \frac{1}{4} =$

4. (E) $\frac{1}{12} \times \frac{1}{5} =$

7. (H) $\frac{3}{4} \times \frac{5}{10} =$

10. (I) $\frac{3}{7} \times \frac{2}{5} =$

2. (N) $\frac{6}{12} \times \frac{1}{8} =$

5. (O) $\frac{9}{10} \times \frac{9}{12} =$

8. (R) $\frac{2}{9} \times \frac{7}{12} =$

11. (S) $\frac{2}{4} \times \frac{3}{8} =$

3. (T) $\frac{1}{7} \times \frac{4}{10} =$

6. (W) $\frac{1}{3} \times \frac{6}{9} =$

9. (Y) $\frac{2}{11} \times \frac{9}{11} =$

Hidden Message

____ ____ ____ , $\frac{6}{35}$ $\frac{2}{35}$ $\frac{3}{16}$ ____ ____ $\frac{1}{6}$ $\frac{3}{16}$ ____ ____ ____ ____ $\frac{1}{60}$ $\frac{1}{6}$ $\frac{3}{16}$ $\frac{18}{121}$

____ ____ $\frac{1}{6}$ $\frac{3}{16}$ ____ ____ ____ , $\frac{27}{40}$ $\frac{1}{16}$ $\frac{1}{60}$ ____ ____ ____ , $\frac{2}{35}$ $\frac{2}{9}$ $\frac{27}{40}$

____ ____ ____ ____ ____ ! $\frac{2}{35}$ $\frac{3}{8}$ $\frac{7}{54}$ $\frac{1}{60}$ $\frac{1}{60}$

MATH SQUARE

Activity
66

Directions

Write each math problem's number under the correct answer.
Each row and column must equal 34. One has been placed for you.

216	81	7	280	
9				→ 34
60	105	270	243	
				→ 34
128	119	78	64	
				→ 34
287	16	8	9	
				→ 34
↓ 34	↓ 34	↓ 34	↓ 34	

MIND-BENDER MATH

1. 4^3 = _____

2. 105 x 1 = _____

3. 56 ÷ 7 = _____

4. 28 ÷ 4 = _____

5. 16 x 8 = _____

6. 3^5 = _____

7. 48 ÷ 3 = _____

8. 41 x 7 = _____

9. 24 x 9 = _216_

10. 9^2 = _____

11. 28 x 10 = _____

12. 10 x 6 = _____

13. 13 x 6 = _____

14. 9 x 30 = _____

15. 17 x 7 = _____

16. 27 ÷ 3 = _____

20 minutes

CITY GRID

Activity
67

MIND-BENDER MATH

Directions

Study the city grid shown below. Notice which numbers are positive and which are negative. Note how the four quadrants are labeled: I, II, III, and IV. Use the information to answer the questions. Remember, always go across before going up or down, and use the point for finding the coordinate.

```
                                      8
      library        park •             7                    mall •
                                      6
                                      5
                                      4
                          •             pet
                        grocery       3   store
                                      2     •
   II                                 1
                                    0
   -8  -7  -6  -5  -4  -3  -2  -1   1   2   3   4   5   6   7   8
                                     -2
          doctor •                           school
                                     -3         •
                                     -4                        o
                                     -5                        f
          bank                                                 f •
            •                        -6                        i
                                     -7     police             c
   III                               -8  IV    •              e
```

1. What feature is located at coordinate (7, 7)? _____

2. What building is located at coordinate (4, -3)? _____

3. What business is located at coordinate (-5, -6)? _____

4. Which quadrant has only negative coordinates? _____

5. Which quadrant has only positive coordinates? _____

6. What coordinate is shown in the police station? _____

7. What building is located at coordinate (-7, 7)? _____

8. What feature is located at coordinate (-2, 7)? _____

5
minutes

Math Trivia

Directions

Answer each math trivia question below.

Activity
68

1. Can a triangle have two right angles? _____

2. How many centimeters are there in three meters? _____

3. What does congruent mean? _____

4. Which weighs more, a pound of feathers or a pound of bricks? _____

5. What are the Roman numerals for 176? _____

6. What instrument is used to measure an angle? _____

7. In the fraction 5/9, which numeral is the numerator? _____

8. How many items are in a gross? _____

9. How many sides does a decagon have? _____

10. What is 6/8 reduced to its lowest terms? _____

11. How many zeros are in one billion? _____

12. Which angle is greater than 90 degrees — obtuse or acute? _____

13. Will perpendicular lines on the same plane ever touch? _____

14. What is the shortest distance between two points? _____

10
minutes

15. Is *fifth* an ordinal or a cardinal number? _____

MIND-BENDER MATH

CALCULATED STORY

Activity
69

Directions

To complete this story, solve the math problems on a calculator and then turn the calculator upside down to read the word. Write the word on the line.

Once upon a time, a girl named _____ broke her
(45,678 – 14,105)

_____ when she fell down a _____.
(123 + 814)   (38,570 ÷ 5)

Her friend _____ came over to say
(9 x 33 + 40)

"_____." _____ brought
(2 + 2 + 10)   (2 x 150 + 37)

_____ an _____. But when
(20,698 + 10,875)   (2,979 ÷ 3)

_____ saw _____ quickly
(989 – 652)   (47,995 – 16,422)

_____ it down, she broke into
(300,000 + 70,000 + 8,800 + 9)

_____. _____ told
(5 x 1,000,000 + 379,919)   (6 x 56 + 1)

_____ , "_____! You're not
(30,000 + 1,000 + 503 + 70)   (9 x 501)

supposed to eat the _____!"
(386,725 ÷ 5)

MIND-BENDER MATH

20 minutes

PUZZLING PATTERNS

Directions

Complete these patterns by filling in the blanks. Each pattern uses two math operations. Then write the rule for each pattern. The first one has been done for you.

1. 2, 5, 11, 23, ___47___ , ___95___ , ___191___ , ___383___

Rule: ___(n × 2) + 1___

2. 3, 10, 31, _____ , _____ , 850, _____ , _____

Rule: _____

3. 1, 6, 26, 106, _____ , _____ , _____ , _____

Rule: _____

4. 1, 2, 7, 32, 157, _____ , _____ , _____ , _____

Rule: _____

5. 1, 8, 36, 148, _____ , _____ , _____ , _____

Rule: _____

6. 4, 11, 32, 95, _____ , _____ , _____ , _____

Rule: _____

7. 1, 5, 33, 229, _____ , _____ , _____ , _____

Rule: _____

8. 5, 13, 29, 61, _____ , _____ , _____ , _____

Rule: _____

9. 7, 15, 31, _____ , 127, _____ , _____ , _____ , _____

Rule: _____

20 minutes

BODY PARTS

Activity

71

Directions

Can you write the names of ten parts of your body that have only three letters in them?

1. _____

2. _____

3. _____

4. _____

5. _____

6. _____

7. _____

8. _____

9. _____

10. _____

BEYOND BRAINY

5 minutes

ODD ONE OUT

Directions

Circle the figure in each group that is different from the others.

1.

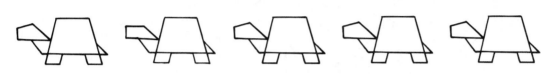

a   b   c   d   e

2.

a   b   c   d   e

3.

a   b   c   d   e

4.

a   b   c   d   e

BEYOND BRAINY

5 minutes

NAMING FUN

Directions

Answer the statements below and circle the 15 answers in the word search.

BEYOND BRAINY

```
H  A  M  H  Y  L  H  N  Q  G  S  Q  H
R  E  B  M  E  T  P  E  S  N  U  N  J
M  T  S  F  R  G  Y  A  W  I  N  U  Z
X  I  A  A  N  R  P  V  I  R  E  E  Y
C  U  E  S  U  L  G  P  V  A  V  W  Q
R  W  V  C  T  O  I  P  F  E  S  T  S
Q  E  R  Z  S  E  L  R  O  H  T  U  R
A  E  B  M  J  U  N  E  P  B  O  W  C
M  E  E  M  S  I  G  H  T  A  U  R  O
M  L  X  V  E  T  I  H  W  S  C  E  V
L  A  L  A  V  V  S  K  V  P  H  D  J
B  G  R  M  N  J  O  D  N  L  Q  L  K
I  H  U  S  A  B  X  N  B  Z  V  Q  S
```

1. Name the two colors of the Canadian flag. _____

2. Name the four months that have exactly 30 days. _____

   _____

3. Name the five senses. _____

   _____

4. Name the four planets closest to the sun. _____

   _____

15 minutes

LICENSE PLATES

Activity
74

Directions

Many license plates are personalized with special messages.
Can you decode the following license plates?

1. | URNIZ |
_____

2. | IM4IT |
_____

3. | BLKNBLU |
_____

4. | LUVNU |
_____

5. | A U |
_____

6. | CR8Z4U |
_____

7. | CRUZN4U |
_____

8. | URBZ |
_____

9. | IM182DAY |
_____

10. | YRUHRE |
_____

11. | BTTRFLI |
_____

12. | PETCHR |
_____

13. | IM4ANTQS |
_____

14. | URAQT |
_____

15. | EZDUZIT |
_____

16. | ICHOT |
_____

BEYOND BRAINY

10 minutes

NAME _____ DATE _____

MAP MADNESS

Activity
75

Directions

Do you see Brandon? He is lost! Follow the directions to get him back on track. Mark his ending spot with an **X**.

Map Directions:

1. Go west on Third Ave.
2. Go left on Peach St.
3. Go left on First Ave.
4. Go left on Plum St.
5. Go east on Fifth Ave.

6. Go right on Pear St.
7. Go left on Second Ave.
8. Go left on Orange St.
9. Go left on Third Ave.
10. End at the corner of Peach St.

BEYOND BRAINY

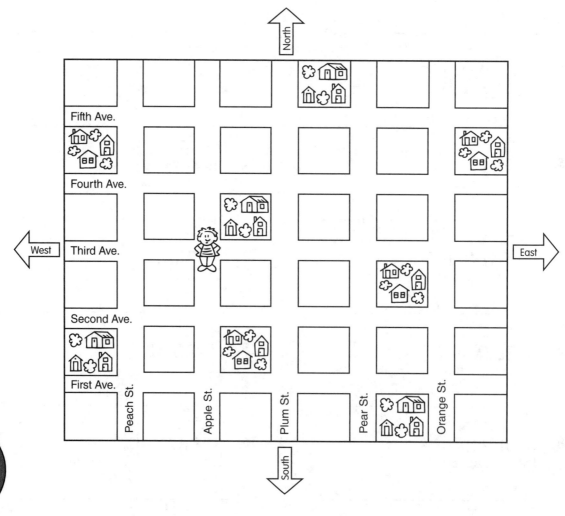

5 minutes

MATCH UP

Activity
76

Directions

The following octagons may look identical at first, but actually they can be divided into four identical pairs. Draw lines to match the identical pairs.

a.
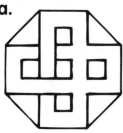

b.
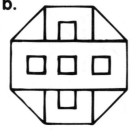

c.
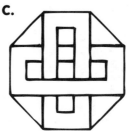

d.
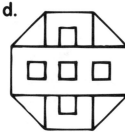

e.
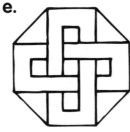

h.
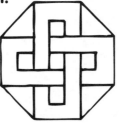

f.
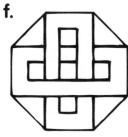

g.
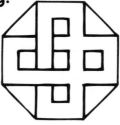

BEYOND BRAINY

5 minutes

TANTALIZING TILES

Activity
11

Directions

Connect the dots to make the pattern below. Then color it
as you wish.

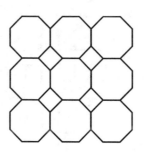

BEYOND BRAINY

10
minutes

REVERSE WORDS

Directions

Reverse words are words that become different words when read backwards. Write the words both forwards and backwards to match the clues below. An example has been done for you.

physician/fish = doc/cod

1. sticky substance/rodent = _____

2. doodle/large hospital room = _____

3. flower container/the best = _____

4. cat and dog/part of staircase = _____

5. not die/cruel = _____

6. not later/opposite of lost = _____

7. half of twenty/tennis court separation = _____

8. shoulder part of a tank top/pieces = _____

9. flying mammals/knife injury = _____

10. pullout from a dresser/prize = _____

11. take a quick look/not give away = _____

12. short rest/used for cooking = _____

13. heavenly body/rodents = _____

14. takes skin off vegetables/nightly rest = _____

15. part of body/hair slicker = _____

BEYOND BRAINY

10 minutes

PICTURE SAYINGS

BEYOND BRAINY

Directions

Sometimes we are able to represent well-known sayings or expressions by illustrating them. Can you figure out the following?

STAND

1. _____

OVER

2. _____

3. _____

4. _____

HOT

5. _____

5 minutes

IDIOMS

Directions

Fill in the blanks with the words in the box to complete the idioms.
Then use the missing words to complete the crossword puzzle.
3 Down has been done for you.

goat
roof
handle
shoulder
crazy
bone
warpath
bed
stack
throat
ceiling

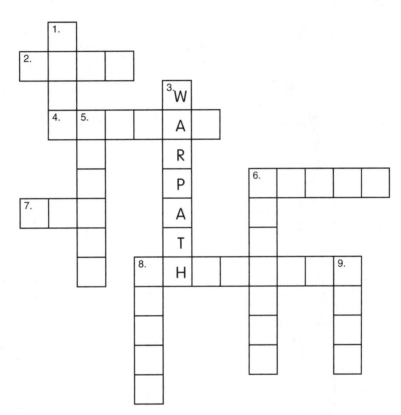

Across

2. Have a _____ to pick with you — to have an argument or try to settle a disagreement with someone

4. Jump down your _____ — to talk or scream at someone in an angry way

6. Drive you _____ — to make someone angry or confused

7. Get up on the wrong side of the _____ — a person is in a bad mood

8. Chip on your _____ — when someone is in a bad mood

Down

1. Get your _____ — to annoy someone and make him or her angry or embarrassed

3. On the ___warpath___ — in a very angry or bad mood, irritated

5. Fly off the _____ — to lose your temper

6. Hit the _____ — to lose your temper suddenly and become very angry

8. Blow your _____ — to lose your temper suddenly and become very angry

9. Hit the _____ — to lose your temper suddenly and become very angry

10 minutes

WHEN IS IT?

Activity
81

Directions

You have received an invitation to a birthday party. The party will be in December, but it is up to you to figure out the actual date. See if you can figure out the date using the clues below.

DECEMBER						
Sun.	Mon.	Tue.	Wed.	Thu.	Fri.	Sat.
		1	2	3	4	5
6	7	8	9	10	11	12
13	14	15	16	17	18	19
20	21	22	23	24	25	26
27	28	29	30	31		

Clues:

- The party is not on Christmas Eve or New Year's Eve.
- The sum of the digits in the date is less than 4.
- The date of the party is not a multiple of 5.
- The party is not on a Monday.
- The digit in the tens place is less than the digit in the ones place.

The birthday party is on _____ , December _____.

(day)   (date)

BEYOND BRAINY

5 minutes

OXYMORONS

Activity 82

Directions

An oxymoron is two words that, when put together, mean the opposite of each other. They are contradictory. Match the words in List A with the words in List B to create an oxymoron. Combine the words together on the lines below. One has been done for you.

List A	
bitter	vaguely
educational	open
sanitary	simply
fresh	paid
half	loud
least	friendly
only	mild
liquid	second
little	industrial
passive	linear

List B	
fire	best
aware	landfill
secret	aggressive
giant	choice
sweet	superb
television	volunteer
frozen	park
naked	librarian
rock	curve
favorite	interest

_____ bitter sweet _____

_____

_____

_____

_____

_____

_____

_____

_____

_____

_____

_____

_____

_____

_____

_____

_____

_____

_____

15 minutes

FAVORITE TEAMS

Activity
8 3

Directions

Five boys root for five different basketball teams. Read the clues to determine which team each likes best. Mark the correct boxes with an **X**.

Clues:

- Will's bedroom is filled with posters and products from the Blazers.
- Brian's father is a big Celtics fan, but Brian is not.
- Chad and Ryan like the Hawks, the Rockets, or the Blazers.
- No boy's favorite team begins with the same letter as his name.

	Celtics	Hawks	Blazers	Rockets	Wizards
Chad					
Henry					
Brian					
Ryan					
Will					

1. Chad's favorite team is the _____.

2. Henry's favorite team is the _____.

3. Brian's favorite team is the _____.

4. Ryan's favorite team is the _____.

10 minutes

5. Will's favorite team is the _____.

BEYOND BRAINY

LETTER PUZZLE

Activity
84

Directions

Nine of these 12 boxes can be used to form a capital letter. Draw the lines within each box where you think it goes below to make the finished puzzle. You may have to erase and redraw the lines a few times. Then write the lowercase letters of the nine boxes you used in the right order.

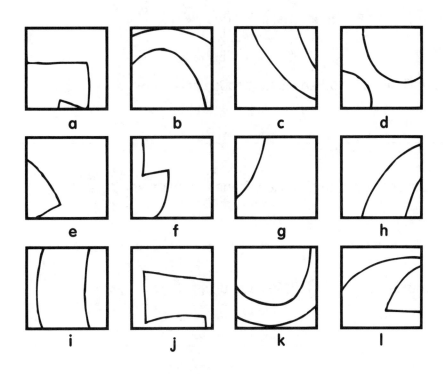

a   b   c   d

e   f   g   h

i   j   k   l

Beyond Brainy

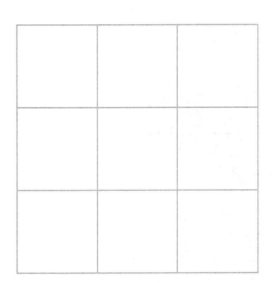

Box Order:

___ ___ ___

___ ___ ___

___ ___ ___

15 minutes

HIDDEN ANIMALS

BEYOND BRAINY

Directions

Hidden in each sentence are three, four, or five animal names. Can you find them? Circle them and write the names on the lines.

Example: Hel p ig l oos! ➜ pig

1. Wait until the pan darkens to add sauce or risk unknown results.

   _____

2. "Isn't baseball amazing?" asked Catherine, her cornea gleaming.

   _____

3. The crowds abhor selfish AM stereo use.

   _____

4. The overcrowded wheelbarrow led to a difficult size brawl.

   _____

5. Is Kristi German, or is Wanda Persian?

   _____

6. "The slob's terrified to bring up pyramids!" said his mother.

   _____

10 minutes

WORD CHAIN

Activity
86

Directions

Fill in each blank with a 3-, 4-, 5-, or 6-letter word, depending on the number of blanks given. Each word must begin with the last letter of the preceding word. The first word may start with any letter. You may use each word only once.

1. _____ _____ _____
2. _____ _____ _____ _____
3. _____ _____ _____ _____ _____ _____
4. _____ _____ _____ _____
5. _____ _____ _____
6. _____ _____ _____
7. _____ _____ _____ _____ _____ _____
8. _____ _____ _____ _____
9. _____ _____ _____ _____
10. _____ _____ _____ _____ _____ _____
11. _____ _____ _____ _____ _____
12. _____ _____ _____
13. _____ _____ _____
14. _____ _____ _____ _____ _____
15. _____ _____ _____ _____
16. _____ _____ _____ _____ _____
17. _____ _____ _____ _____ _____ _____
18. _____ _____ _____ _____
19. _____ _____ _____ _____ _____
20. _____ _____ _____ _____

BEYOND BRAINY

10 minutes

HIDDEN MEANINGS

Activity
87

Directions

Explain the meaning of each box.

FACE / ꟻACƎ	$\dfrac{0}{\text{B.S.} \ \text{M.A.} \ \text{Ph.D.}}$	k c e h c
1. _____	5. _____	9. _____
LE VEL	sota	**Man** Campus
2. _____	6. _____	10. _____
$\dfrac{\text{HEAD}}{\text{HEELS}}$	$\dfrac{\text{GROUND}}{\text{FT FT / FT FT / FT FT}}$	little little late late
3. _____	7. _____	11. _____
coORDERurt	YOUjustMe	School
4. _____	8. _____	12. _____

15 minutes

BEYOND BRAINY

WORKING WITH CODES

Directions

Codes are made using patterns of numbers and letters. Good "code crackers" become very good at noticing patterns. Study these codes, complete them, and decode the messages.

1.

	20	21										
A	B	C	D	E	F	G	H	I	J	K	L	M
								14	15			
N	O	P	Q	R	S	T	U	V	W	X	Y	Z

Message: 12 19 3 23 11 26 23 4 12 23 10 13 6 12 1 4 24 13 10 12 26 23 10 6 7 12 1 21 23

Decode: _____

_____

2.

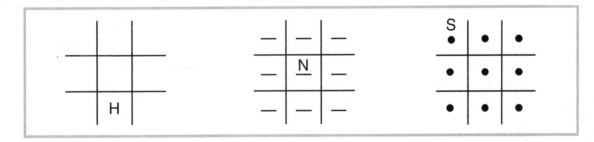

Message:

Decode: _____

_____

15 minutes

Changing Letters

Directions

Change the letters in the starting clue by following the directions below. When moving letters, the remaining letters will move over. When you finish, you will reveal the name of the U.S. president the clue refers to.

Starting Clue: FIRST TO FLY IN PLANE

BEYOND BRAINY

1. Swap the first and fifth letters.

   __ __ __ __ __ __ __ __ __ __ __ __ __ __ __

2. Move the last letter to the second position.

   __ __ __ __ __ __ __ __ __ __ __ __ __ __ __

3. Delete the last two letters.

   __ __ __ __ __ __ __ __ __ __ __ __ __

4. Move the seventh letter to the last position.

   __ __ __ __ __ __ __ __ __ __ __ __ __

5. Move the tenth letter to the fifth position.

   __ __ __ __ __ __ __ __ __ __ __ __ __

6. Delete each I.

   __ __ __ __ __ __ __ __ __ __ __

7. Double the O.

   __ __ __ __ __ __ __ __ __ __ __ __

8. Move the R to the sixth position.

   __ __ __ __ __ __ __ __ __ __ __ __

9. Delete all Fs.

   __ __ __ __ __ __ __ __ __ __ __

10. Add two Ds between the second and third letters.

    __ __ __ __ __ __ __ __ __ __ __ __ __

11. Move S after the second O.

    __ __ __ __ __ __ __ __ __ __ __ __ __

12. Delete the third, fourth, and fifth letters from the right.

    __ __ __ __ __ __ __ __ __ __

13. Add the word EVE between the S and the L.

    __ __ __ __ __ __ __ __ __ __ __ __ __

15 minutes

CAR RALLY

Directions

The Car Rally has been sabotaged! Choose the correct piece to put back into the directions to lead the competitors safely across the uncharted lands.

CAR RALLY DIRECTIONS

Start 4E, 2N, ⟨　　　⟩2N,
2W,⟨　5E, 2N, 3NW,
2N, 3SE, 3E,⟩1N, 4E, 2N,
4NW,⟨　　Finish

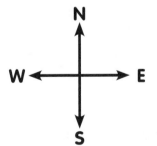

a. ⟨2W, 4N, 3E,⟩
⟨2N, 4E, 10S,
⟨2N, 4W,
NW, 2S

b. ⟨2W, 4N, 5E,⟩
⟨2N, 4W, 11S,
3N, 1E,
2NW, 2E⟩

c. ⟨2W, 4N, 5E,⟩
⟨2N, 4E, 11S,
3N, 1W,
2NE, 2SE⟩

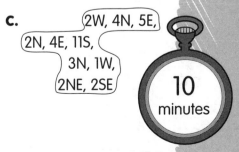

10 minutes

                                       #2940 101 Activities for Fast Finishers

AROUND THE ISLAND

BEYOND BRAINY

Directions

Juan flew around the island in 95 hours. But which route did he take? Start from "M" on the map and fly west to "A," and then continue around the island. Your flight must take exactly 95 hours.

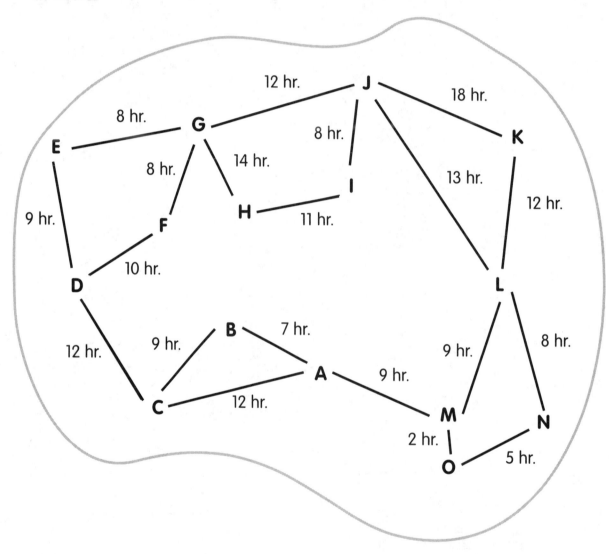

List the order of Juan's flight: __M, A,_____

_____

15
minutes

NAME _____   DATE _____

STEP BY STEP

Activity
92

Directions

You can change "blunt" into "sharp" in 13 steps! Read each clue then change just one letter of the previous answer to make the new word.

B	L	U	N	T	
					the main force or effect of
					a low, pig-like noise
					let have
					$1,000
					products made by the same company
					has no taste or flavor
					empty, not written in
					a straight length of wood
					to put seeds in the ground
					not level
					abbreviation of "shall not"
					boy's name
					to give out a fair portion
S	H	A	R	P	

Beyond Brainy

10 minutes

COLORFUL PUZZLERS

Activity 93

Directions

Match the colorful phrases in the box with the appropriate descriptors.

_____ 1. beverage

_____ 2. a space place

_____ 3. salad dressing

_____ 4. a dessert

_____ 5. termite

_____ 6. really tall tree

_____ 7. type of bee

_____ 8. nursery rhyme

_____ 9. cookie ingredient

_____ 10. name of a country

_____ 11. polar mammal

_____ 12. "caught in the act"

_____ 13. proceed ahead

_____ 14. bruised

_____ 15. football team

_____ 16. warning in soccer

_____ 17. infection

_____ 18. "hot" fruit

_____ 19. no electricity

_____ 20. flowers

_____ 21. path in Wizard of Oz

_____ 22. signal of surrender

_____ 23. structure for growing plants

_____ 24. a notice of dismissal

A. white flag	**I.** redwood	**Q.** greenhouse
B. white ant	**J.** pinkeye	**R.** green light
C. white bear	**K.** pink slip	**S.** yellow brick road
D. black and blue	**L.** pink lemonade	**T.** yellow card
E. black hole	**M.** "Little Boy Blue"	**U.** yellow jacket
F. blackouts	**N.** blue cheese	**V.** brownie
G. red chili pepper	**O.** bluebells	**W.** brown sugar
H. red-handed	**P.** Greenland	**X.** Browns

15 minutes

Boggle the Mind

Directions

Look at the letters in the grids below. How many words can you think of using these letters? Follow the rules below to find your answers.

Rules:

- You must use the central letter of the grid as the beginning of each word.
- No letter can be used more than once in the same word.
- Letters do not need to be connected.
- No proper nouns or slang words allowed.

1.

F	T	O
E	**L**	S
A	M	N

Words

2.

K	L	I
N	**M**	A
T	U	S

Words

3.

E	N	I
U	**T**	R
M	A	Y

Words

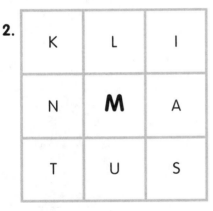

15 minutes

BEYOND BRAINY

THE BIG RACE

Activity
95

Directions

Jack, Amy, Eric, and Kelly ran a race while wearing different-colored shirts. Read each clue. Then mark the chart to see where each kid finished in the race and which shirt he or she wore. Mark the correct boxes with **X**s.

Clues:

✔ Neither of the boys finished first or last.
✔ Neither the person wearing yellow nor the person wearing green finished first or second.
✔ Amy didn't finish fourth, and she didn't wear blue.
✔ Jack finished ahead of Eric.
✔ Eric didn't wear green.

	Green	Blue	Red	Yellow	First	Second	Third	Fourth
Jack								
Amy								
Eric								
Kelly								

1. What color did Jack wear? How did he finish? _____

2. What color did Amy wear? How did she finish? _____

3. What color did Eric wear? How did he finish? _____

4. What color did Kelly wear? How did she finish? _____

BEYOND BRAINY

10 minutes

CODED MESSAGE

Directions

Circle the correct letter for each problem below. Then take the circled letter and write it in the corresponding blank in order to reveal a famous saying.

$\overline{}\ \overline{}\ \overline{}$ $\overline{}\ \overline{}\ \overline{}$ $\overline{}\ \overline{}$ $\overline{}\ \overline{}\ \overline{}$
    7   2   6   8   5   3   11   1   7   2   6

$\overline{}\ \overline{}\ \overline{}\ \overline{}\ \overline{}$ $\overline{}\ \overline{}\ \overline{}$ $\overline{}\ \overline{}\ \overline{}$
    9   4   11   3   10   7   2   6   8   5   3

1. If a person walked on the moon in 1492, circle S. If not, circle F.

2. If a prairie dog is a dog, circle K. If it is a rodent, circle O.

3. If your father's sister is your aunt, circle N. If not, circle A.

4. If 6 x 9 = 55, circle M. If not, circle H.

5. If antonyms are words that mean the opposite of one another, circle A. If not, circle L.

6. If Brazil is a country in Europe, circle K. If not, circle U.

7. If the capital of Illinois is Springfield, circle Y. If not, circle U.

8. If the trumpet is a woodwind instrument, circle Z. If not, circle C.

9. If J.K. Rowling wrote *Harry Potter*, circle T. If not, circle W.

10. If a telescope is used to view things far away, circle K. If not, circle M.

11. If the Statue of Liberty is located in Washington, D.C., circle E. If not, circle I.

BASEBALL EQUATIONS

Activity 97

Directions

Each equation below contains the first letters of words that will make it complete and explain how the number relates to baseball. Write the missing words. The first one has been done for you.

BEYOND BRAINY

1. 9 = the number of P _____players_____ on a B ___baseball___ T ____team____

2. 90 = the number of F _____ between B _____

3. 3 = the number of S _____ that make an O _____

4. 0 = the number of H _____ in a N _____ -H _____

5. 9 = the number of I _____ in a G_____

6. 4 = the number of R _____ for a G _____ S _____

7. 7 = the number of G _____ in the W _____ S _____

8. 14 = the number of T _____ in the A _____ L _____

9. 16 = the number of T _____ in the N _____ L _____

10. 5 = the number of S _____ on H _____ P _____

11. 4 = the number of B _____ that make a W_____

12. 5 ounces = the W _____ of a B _____

13. 4 = the number of U _____ per G _____

14. 1 = the number of M _____ per T _____

10 minutes

WORD WINDERS

Activity
98

Directions

Use the clues to help you fill in the blanks and circles. Only the circled letters change from one word to the next. The first two have been done for you. (Note: When a word has fewer spaces than the word above it, simply drop the letter above the empty space.)

1. pointed   s h a r p

2. a fish that can be dangerous   s h a r (k)

3. to use together

4. to be concerned

5. a navigator's map

6. to delight

7. not soft

8. synonym for rabbit

9. money paid to ride a bus

10. land used to raise crops

11. a signal used to give warning

12. a small songbird

13. the sound a dog makes

14. without light

15. to have sufficient courage

16. a fruit

17. after the usual time

18. a bowling alley

19. a walking stick

20. a wafer for holding ice cream

21. finished

BEYOND BRAINY

15
minutes

PRESIDENTIAL PUNS

Activity
99

Directions

A pun is a funny play on words. Use the names of the past U.S. presidents in the box to answer these presidential puns. Not all presidents listed will be used.

Madison	Cleveland	Garfield	Polk
Hoover	Washington	Fillmore	Bush
Harding	Coolidge	Nixon	Grant
Taylor	Pierce	Monroe	Truman

1. Which president was the most honest? _____

2. Which president often jabbed at others? _____

3. Which president was irritated by his child? _____

4. Which president was popular at a gas station? _____

5. Which president was the namesake of a popular cat? _____

6. Which president sewed clothing? _____

7. Which president took care of the laundry? _____

8. Which president enjoyed landscaping? _____

9. Which president was often cold? _____

10. Which president vacuumed the carpets? _____

11. Which president gave permission for everything? _____

12. Which president loved earrings? _____

10 minutes

BEYOND BRAINY

GEOGRAPHY SANDWICHES

Directions

Sandwiches are made with two pieces of bread and a filling in the middle. In these geography sandwiches, you are given the "bread" but not the "filling." Study a map of the United States to make the proper sandwiches below. (Note: Not all "fillings" are states.)

1. Mississippi _____ Georgia

2. North Dakota _____ Nebraska

3. Wisconsin _____ Michigan

4. New York _____ Rhode Island

5. Oklahoma _____ Texas

6. California _____ Utah

7. Texas _____ Mexico

8. Illinois _____ Ohio

9. Arizona _____ Texas

10. Missouri _____ Illinois

11. Canada _____ Mexico

12. Vermont _____ Maine

13. Minnesota _____ Missouri

14. Pacific Ocean _____ Nevada

15. Washington _____ California

BEYOND BRAINY

10 minutes

HIGHEST SCORE

Activity

101

Directions

Find the highest score you can out of five tries following the rules below. Circle your highest score and color in that path on the grid.

Rules

- You must start on a number on the top row.

- You must finish on a number on the bottom row.

- You can make only 20 moves.

- Each move may only be vertical or horizontal.

- Add the numbers as you move. Record your tries below.

2	7	9	6	1	4	8	2
8	3	5	7	2	5	0	4
7	0	8	2	9	6	3	8
2	3	5	0	1	3	7	5
5	1	4	6	9	4	0	2
6	8	2	7	3	9	4	6
1	9	0	5	4	0	3	8
2	7	3	8	1	6	9	1

1st Try: _____

2nd Try: _____

3rd Try: _____

4th Try: _____

5th Try: _____

20
minutes

BEYOND BRAINY

Answer Key

Activity 1
1. Row 5
2. T
3. E
4. Row 6
5. Rows 4 and 5
6. mate, meat, tame, team

Activity 2
1. A　　　8. A
2. A　　　9. S
3. S　　　10. X
4. X　　　11. S
5. S　　　12. S
6. S　　　13. S
7. X　　　14. A

Activity 3
1. lawn
2. heel
3. hole
4. whale

Mystery Word: Halloween
5. cut
6. clap
7. canoe

Mystery Word: cantaloupe

Activity 4
Answers will vary.
Possibilities include: ape, are, bare, bean, beam, bear, beg, bet, blew, brew, feal, fear, felt, fern, few, flew, gear, gem, get, grape, grew, hear, heart, heat, help, lame, lane, lean, leap, male, mane, mare, mean, meat, met, net, pear, peg, pen, pet, real, rent, table, tame, team, tear, ten, wear, web, wept, when

Activity 5
1. eagle　　7. perfect
2. jewel　　8. coffee
3. fence　　9. member
4. general　10. gentle
5. enemy　11. enter
6. velvet　12. pretend

Activity 6
Answers will vary.
Possibilities include: cable, canoe, carve, cause, cease, chafe, chose, chide, chime, chive, choke, chore, chose, clone, close, clove, coupe, crate, crave, crepe, crime, crude, curse, curve, cycle

Activity 7
1. raise
2. sit or lie
3. lie or sit
4. sitting
5. lays, lay
6. rising, setting
7. rise
8. lying
9. sat
10. raised

Activity 8
1. chemist
2. surveyor
3. builder
4. architect
5. watchmaker
6. bricklayer
7. teacher
8. jeweler
9. carpenter
10. plumber
11. farmer
12. dentist
13. driving instructor
14. lawyer
15. hairdresser
16. secretary

Activity 9
1. shoes
2. coats
3. bread

Activity 10
1. clean　　11. broken
2. best　　12. close
3. agreed　13. action
4. fast　　14. dark
5. catch　15. deep
6. beautiful　16. always
7. exciting　17. determine
8. behind　18. edge
9. done　　19. difficult
10. below　20. expect

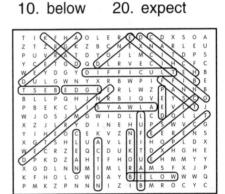

Activity 11
Across　　　　Down
1. grow　　　1. gift
2. go　　　　2. gave
3. get　　　　3. guess
5. general　　4. glance
7. harm　　　5. guilty
8. gain　　　6. handy
10. heavy　　9. hairy
11. happy　　10. heard
12. here　　　12. hit
13. grief
14. great

ANSWER KEY (cont.)

Activity 12
1. helping: is
   action: raising
2. helping: has
   action: learned
3. helping: is
   action: drawing
4. helping: will
   action: drink
5. helping: has
   action: taken
6. helping: have
   action: seen
7. helping: are
   action: going
8. helping: can
   action: ride
9. helping: will
   action: eat

Activity 13
Correctly spelled words:
anchor, envelope, assistant, accident, general, already, leopard, separate, frown, usually, soldier, answer, lizard, easily, robust, danger, careful, friend, benefit, tomorrow, schedule

Activity 14
Possibilities include: resting, rests, assisting, assign, assists, coasting, coasts, coach, coats, rusting, rusts, ruts, trusting, trusts, truck, trumpet, truth, listing, lists, lick, disgusting, disguise, disgusts, crusting, crusts, crumpet, boasting, boasts, boats, promise

Activity 15
1. magpie
2. ostrich
3. monkey, donkey
4. parrot
5. porcupine
6. bat, cat, rat, goat
7. trout
8. mouse
9. toucan, pelican
10. butterfly, dragonfly

Activity 16
Nouns: envelope, Betsy Ross, apron, father
Verbs: eating, jumped, read, sleep
Pronouns: she, it, they, we
Conjunctions: so, and, but, yet
Adverbs: happily, joyfully, furiously, softly
Adjectives: thin, twenty, red, pretty

Activity 17
1. rag, fragile
2. act, factory
3. ear, dreary
4. in, pink
5. ill, million
6. last, elastic
7. chest, orchestra
8. name, enamel

Activity 18
1. time
2. mare
3. chair
4. tame
5. team
6. heart
7. cream
8. rat
9. tear
10. math
11. meat
12. heat

Activity 19
1. bananas
2. biscuits
3. cheese
4. chicken
5. coffee
6. margarine
7. mustard
8. sauce
9. sausages
10. steak

Activity 20
1. turnip
2. python
3. almond
4. wallet
5. hamper
6. desert
7. twelve
8. marble
9. stable
10. banana

Activity 21
1. wax
2. guard
3. squash
4. buckle
5. plug
6. school
7. pinch
8. touched

Activity 22
call/cane: candle, calves, candy, camel
canine/cattle: category, caramel, canopy, capable
caution/cement: cave, celebrate, celery, ceiling
center/certain: centimeter, cereal, ceremony, century

Activity 23
1. capital
2. bear
3. passed
4. it's
5. Who's
6. led
7. peace
8. their, two
9. fair, fare
10. right, write, rite
11. patience, patients
12. dessert, desert

Activity 24
1. campground
2. pancake
3. lookout
4. doghouse
5. toothpaste
6. sandbox
7. grandmother

ANSWER KEY (cont.)

Activity 24 (cont.)
8. overboard
9. ladybug
10. thumbtack
11. handshake
12. flowerpot
13. handbag
14. thumbprint
15. sandstorm
16. pigpen
17. bedtime

Activity 25
1. desert
2. capital
3. thorough
4. anyway
5. effect
6. imply
7. latter
8. angel
9. illicit
10. disprove
11. stationery
12. accept
13. proceed
14. preposition
15. quit

Activity 26
1. "I don't want any nasty pigeons roosting on my Ford pickup," said my father.
2. We are camping and going hiking in the desert for the Memorial Day weekend.
3. Rosa bought peaches, grapes, and apricots when she went to the supermarket.
4. My favorite pies are made with rhubarb and gooseberries. They are sweet and sour.
5. My mother was born on February 14, 1970, in New Orleans, Louisiana.
6. My father is from the state of Maine, and he is stationed in Portland with the U.S. Coast Guard.
7. Using a word processor can be helpful for both the beginning and the experienced writer.
8. Maria's van died twice on the freeway, and she decided to buy a new car.

Activity 27
Answers will vary.
Possibilities include:
1. Undri is always late; for example, he was 30 minutes late to class yesterday.
2. Mr. Yates introduced the speaker; afterwards, he sat down.
3. The construction crew could not get the materials; consequently, they could not finish the job.
4. Tory became tired of doing her sister's work; meanwhile, she had her own work to do.
5. Welton did not dislike the movie; in fact, he enjoyed it immensely.
6. Zenia missed the first bus; however, she arrived on time.
7. Vladimir always follows instructions; as a result, he makes good grades.

Activity 28
Answers will vary. Accept appropriate responses.

Activity 29
4, 1, 3, 5, 2, 6

Activity 30
1. Chores
2. Favorite Foods
3. School
4. Pet Peeves
5. Ice Cream
6. Homework
7. Favorite Rides
8. Travel
9. Summer
10. Sports

Activity 31
1. declare   7. F
2. biannual   8. B
3. predict   9. E
4. dictator   10. C
5. veep   11. A
6. reform   12. D

Activity 32
1. d
2. b
3. a

Activity 33
1. c   3. b
2. b   4. c

Activity 34
1. d   3. c
2. a   4. d

Activity 35
Answers will vary. Accept appropriate responses.

ANSWER KEY (cont.)

Activity 36

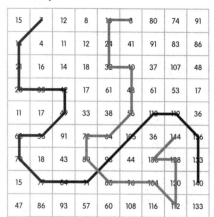

Activity 37
There are 20 triangles.

Activity 38
1. $1.45   6. $3.55
2. $1.45   7. $3.20
3. $2.75   8. $2.40
4. $2.10   9. $3.25
5. $2.60   10. $3.35

Activity 39
Check drawings for accuracy.

Activity 40

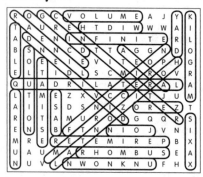

Activity 41
Answers will vary.

Activity 42
the number sign (or pound sign)
#

Activity 43

1.
5	0	4
2	3	4
2	6	1
(9)

2.
8	7	3
1	6	11
9	5	4
(18)

3.
3	3	6
7	4	1
2	5	5
(12)

4.
5	13	3
5	7	9
11	1	9
(21)

5.
8	3	4
1	5	9
6	7	2
(15)

6.
9	15	6
7	10	13
14	5	11
(30)

Activity 44
1. 23   3. 16
2. 3   4. 75

Activity 45
1. Row C   4. Row F
2. Row D   5. Row B
3. Row C

Activity 46

1.
4	1	5	3	2
1	26	3	23	3
3	5	4	2	1
5	25	2	23	4
2	3	1	4	5

2.
4	1	3	2	5
2	22	1	20	3
5	4	2	3	1
1	28	4	22	4
3	4	5	1	2

3.
5	4	2	3	1
3	25	1	21	5
1	5	4	3	2
4	25	3	27	4
2	1	5	3	4

4.
2	3	4	1	5
4	20	1	25	3
1	3	2	5	4
5	26	3	24	2
3	4	5	2	1

Activity 47
STEAL ITS CHAIR

Activity 48
1. f   5. g
2. e   6. c
3. d   7. 9,020
4. a   8. 21,432

Activity 49

1.
5	1	6	4	2	8	3	9	7
7	4	3	6	9	1	5	2	8
8	2	9	5	3	7	1	4	6
3	8	7	9	6	5	2	1	4
9	5	4	8	1	2	6	7	3
2	6	1	7	4	3	9	8	5
6	7	8	1	5	9	4	3	2
4	9	2	3	8	6	7	5	1
1	3	5	2	7	4	8	6	9

2.
3	1	4	2	8	5	6	9	7
5	9	8	6	4	7	1	3	2
7	6	2	3	9	1	4	5	8
9	8	3	1	7	4	2	6	5
2	4	5	8	3	6	7	1	9
1	7	6	9	5	2	3	8	4
4	3	7	5	1	8	9	2	6
8	2	1	4	6	9	5	7	3
6	5	9	7	2	3	8	4	1

3.
8	6	2	4	7	1	5	9	3
4	7	3	5	2	9	6	8	1
5	1	9	8	3	6	4	2	7
9	3	8	1	4	5	7	6	2
7	4	1	2	6	8	3	5	9
2	5	6	7	9	3	1	4	8
6	9	5	3	1	2	8	7	4
3	2	7	6	8	4	9	1	5
1	8	4	9	5	7	2	3	6

4.
7	6	4	8	2	5	9	1	3
9	5	2	4	1	3	7	6	8
3	1	8	9	6	7	2	4	5
8	7	5	2	9	1	6	3	4
6	2	3	5	4	8	1	7	9
1	4	9	7	3	6	5	8	2
5	8	6	3	7	2	4	9	1
4	3	1	6	5	9	8	2	7
2	9	7	1	8	4	3	5	6

Activity 50
Answers will vary.

Activity 51

1.
2	9	5	7	23
3	6	1	4	14
6	3	2	9	20
5	9	7	2	23
16	27	15	22	

2.
4	9	3	9	25
1	5	4	7	17
2	2	5	3	12
3	4	2	6	15
10	20	14	25	

3.
3	8	6	2	9	28
9	6	3	3	5	26
1	2	2	2	2	9
9	8	5	7	3	32
7	5	2	8	4	26
29	29	18	22	23	

4.
3	4	2	5	7	21
7	6	4	1	4	22
5	1	6	3	2	17
3	9	6	8	3	29
2	4	7	8	2	23
20	24	25	25	18	

Activity 52
1. 8 quarters, 2 nickels, 1 penny
2. 2 half dollars, 8 quarters, 3 pennies
3. 4 half dollars, 2 quarters, 7 dimes, 7 pennies
4. 18 quarters, 1 penny
5. 7 half dollars, 1 quarter, 4 nickels, 2 pennies

Activity 53
1. 3 x 2 + 4 = 10
2. 8 + 8 − 6 = 10
3. 20 ÷ 5 + 4 = 8
4. 12 − 4 x 2 = 16
5. 14 + 6 + 10 = 30
6. 20 − 4 − 6 = 10
7. 5 x 3 + 5 = 20
8. 30 ÷ 6 + 12 = 17
9. 40 − 20 − 20 = 0
10. 7 + 7 x 2 = 28

Activity 54

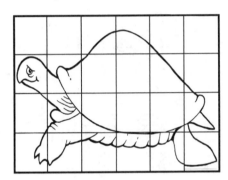

Activity 55
Section A: red, 3
Section B: orange, 2
Section C: yellow, 8
Section D: green, 5
Section E: blue, 6
Section F: purple, 7

Activity 56
1. 60, 50, 10, 50, 300
2. 140, 280, 780, 260, 2,600
3. 48, 96, 24, 12, 36
4. 1,500, 500, 250, 125, 25

Activity 57
1. 941,093
2. 8,276,935

Activity 58
1. 187 − 91 ÷ 8 x 6 + 3 = 75
2. 210 x 4 + 105 − 45 ÷ 30 = 30
3. 64 ÷ 4 x 8 − 105 + 110 = 133
4. 104 − 33 + 61 x 4 ÷ 8 = 66
5. 64 + 77 ÷ 3 x 9 − 99 = 324
6. 76 x 4 + 84 ÷ 2 − 194 = 0
7. 77 − 12 x 6 ÷ 10 + 31 = 70
8. 47 + 109 − 83 x 6 ÷ 6 = 73

Activity 59
TEN MINUTES FREE PLAY!

Activity 60
Across	Down
1. 444	1. 42
4. 47	2. 4,685
6. 2,608	3. 404
7. 84	5. 733
8. 63	8. 6,245
9. 55	9. 563
10. 2,544	11. 56
13. 32	12. 49
14. 659	

Activity 61
834 ÷ 417 = 348 ÷ 174
117 ÷ 39 = 18 ÷ 6
224 ÷ 56 = 268 ÷ 67
225 ÷ 45 = 984 − 979
6 x 24 = 8 x 18
17 x 32 = 8 x 68
13 x 28 = 14 x 26
14 x 44 = 22 x 28
9 x 72 = 6 x 108
15 x 43 = 5 x 129
534 ÷ 89 = 402 ÷ 67
19 x 15 = 3 x 95
9 x 7 = 504 ÷ 8
4 + 3 = 259 ÷ 37
358 + 872 = 243 + 987

Activity 62
Across	Down
1. 382,600	1. 307,597
2. 516,519	3. 135,864
5. 133,110	4. 332,760
9. 145,640	6. 136,686
10. 746,504	7. 346,255
12. 225,446	8. 276,416
14. 105,322	11. 123,024
15. 29,580	13. 610,176
16. 445,842	16. 483,720
17. 748,979	
18. 271,759	

Activity 63
5,776	1,189	4,118	2,356	1,173	1,548	6,820	1,029	704	Finish
1,073	361	899	226	1,955	266	1,615	901	1,209	897
915	1,116	6,631	4,059	1,360	5,643	1,736	5,889	745	158
713	810	901	760	584	2,410	602	585	345	6,105
5,615	1,196	799	1,411	1,222	6,760	609	1,404	1,027	319
713	2,002	801	189	1,177	986	1,612	605	884	2,957
1,020	2,429	1,380	570	3,384	522	1,099	946	625	157
1,037	737	979	1,003	2,920	1,564	530	697	539	811
578	246	623	1,131	409	818	794	376	263	7,057
121	1,792	963	219	304	1,102	4,112	2,876	3,006	914

Activity 64
Across	Down
1. two	1. three
4. four	2. one
5. ten	3. four
6. three	4. five
9. nine	5. two
11. two	6. three
13. seven	7. eight
14. six	8. six
	10. five
	12. one
	13. six
	14. seven

Activity 65
1. 1/6	7. 3/8
2. 1/16	8. 7/54
3. 2/35	9. 18/121
4. 1/60	10. 6/35
5. 27/40	11. 3/16
6. 2/9	

IT'S AS EASY AS ONE, TWO, THREE!

ANSWER KEY (cont.)

Activity 66

216	81	7	280
9	10	4	11	→ 34
60	105	270	243
12	2	14	6	→ 34
128	119	78	64
5	15	13	1	→ 34
287	16	8	9
8	7	3	16	→ 34

↓ 34 ↓ 34 ↓ 34 ↓ 34

1. 64	9. 216
2. 105	10. 81
3. 8	11. 280
4. 7	12. 60
5. 128	13. 78
6. 243	14. 270
7. 16	15. 119
8. 287	16. 9

Activity 67
1. mall
2. school
3. bank
4. III
5. I
6. (3, -8)
7. library
8. park

Activity 68
1. no
2. 300
3. equal shape and size
4. they weigh the same
5. CLXXVI
6. protractor
7. 5
8. 12 dozen, or 144
9. 10
10. 3/4
11. 9
12. obtuse
13. yes
14. a straight line
15. ordinal

Activity 69
Once upon a time, a girl named <u>Elsie</u> broke her <u>leg</u> when she fell down a <u>hill</u>. Her friend <u>Lee</u> came over to say "<u>hi</u>." <u>Lee</u> brought <u>Elsie</u> an <u>egg</u>. But when <u>Lee</u> saw <u>Elsie</u> quickly <u>gobble</u> it down, she broke into <u>giggles</u>. <u>Lee</u> told <u>Elsie</u>, "<u>Gosh</u>! You're not supposed to eat the <u>shell</u>!"

Activity 70
1. 47; 95; 191; 383;
   Rule: (n x 2) + 1
2. 94; 283; 850; 2,551, 7654;
   Rule: (n x 3) + 1
3. 426; 1,706; 6,826, 27,306;
   Rule: (n x 4) + 2
4. 782; 3,907; 19,532; 97,657;
   Rule: (n x 5) – 3
5. 596; 2,388; 9,556; 38,228;
   Rule: (n x 4) + 4
6. 284; 851; 2,552; 7,655;
   Rule: (n x 3) – 1
7. 1,601; 11,205; 78,433; 549,029;
   Rule: (n x 7) – 2
8. 125; 253; 509; 1,021;
   Rule: (n x 2) + 3
9. 63; 127; 255; 511; 1,023;, 2,047;
   Rule: (n x 2) + 1

Activity 71
arm, ear, eye, gum, hip, jaw, leg, lip, rib, toe (gut, lid)

Activity 72
1. b
2. d
3. a
4. c

Activity 73
1. red, white
2. April, June, September, November
3. sight, hearing, touch, taste, smell
4. Mercury, Venus, Earth, Mars

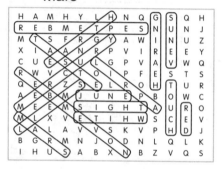

Activity 74
1. You are nice.
2. I'm for it.
3. Black and Blue
4. Lovin' You
5. Hey You!
6. Crazy for You
7. Cruisin' for You
8. You are busy.
9. I'm 18 today.
10. Why are you here?
11. Butterfly
12. P.E. Teacher
13. I'm for Antiques
14. You're a Cutie
15. Easy Does It
16. Icy Hot

ANSWER KEY (cont.)

Activity 75

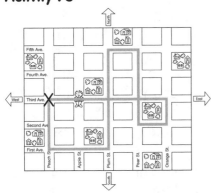

Activity 76
Identical pairs:
a and g
b and d
c and f
e and h

Activity 77
Check drawing for accuracy.

Activity 78
1. tar/rat
2. draw/ward
3. pot/top
4. pets/step
5. live/evil
6. now/won
7. ten/net
8. strap/parts
9. bats/stab
10. drawer/reward
11. peek/keep
12. nap/pan
13. star/rats
14. peels/sleep
15. leg/gel

Activity 79
1. I understand
2. over the rainbow
3. raining cats and dogs
4. tap dance
5. hot under the collar

Activity 80
Across
2. bone
4. throat
6. crazy
7. bed
8. shoulder

Down
1. goat
3. warpath
5. handle
6. ceiling
8. stack
9. roof

Activity 81
The birthday party is on Saturday, December 12.

Activity 82
bitter sweet
sanitary landfill
fresh frozen
liquid rock
passive aggressive
paid volunteer
educational television
half naked
least favorite
little giant
only choice
industrial park
second best
simply superb
mild interest
linear curve
friendly fire
vaguely aware
open secret
loud librarian

Activity 83
1. Chad: Rockets
2. Henry: Celtics
3. Brian: Wizards
4. Ryan: Hawks
5. Will: Blazers

Activity 84
Box Order:
Row 1: h, b, e
Row 2: i, j, a
Row 3: c, k, g

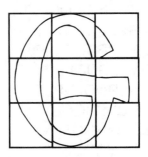

Activity 85
1. panda, toad, skunk
2. llama, cat, eagle
3. crow, horse, fish, hamster
4. crow, eel, owl, toad, zebra
5. tiger, swan, ape
6. lobster, guppy, ram, moth

Activity 86
Answers will vary.

Activity 87
1. face to face
2. split level
3. head over heels
4. order in the court
5. 3 degrees below zero
6. Minnesota
7. 6 feet under ground
8. just between you and me
9. check up
10. big man on campus
11. too little too late
12. high school

Activity 88
1. Take shelter until further notice.
2. Unable to find suitable hideaway.

ANSWER KEY (cont.)

Activity 89
1. TIRSFTOFLYINPLANE
2. TEIRSFTOFLYINPLAN
3. TEIRSFTOFLYINPL
4. TEIRSFOFLYINPLT
5. TEIRYSFOFLINPLT
6. TERYSFOFLNPLT
7. TERYSFOOFLNPLT
8. TEYSFROOFLNPLT
9. TEYSROOLNPLT
10. TEDDYSROOLNPLT
11. TEDDYROOSLNPLT
12. TEDDYROOSLT
13. TEDDYROOSEVELT

Activity 90
Choice c

Activity 91
M, A, B, C, D, F, G, J, L, N, O, M

Activity 92
BLUNT, brunt, grunt, grant, grand, brand, bland, blank, plank, plant, slant, shan't, Shane, share, SHARP

Activity 93
1.	L	13.	R
2.	E	14.	D
3.	N	15.	X
4.	V	16.	T
5.	B	17.	J
6.	I	18.	G
7.	U	19.	F
8.	M	20.	O
9.	W	21.	S
10.	P	22.	A
11.	C	23.	Q
12.	H	24.	K

Activity 94
Answers will vary.
Possibilities include:
1. lame, lament, lane, lanes, late, leaf, lean, leans, left, lefts, let, lets, loaf, loft, lofts, lone, lose, lost, lot, lots
2. mail, main, malt, malts, man, mask, mast, mat, mats, maul, milk, milks, mink, minks, mist, must
3. tame, tamer, tan, tar, tea, team, tear, teary, ten, tier, time, timer, tiny, tire, train, tram, tray, trim, true, try, tuna, tune, turn

Activity 95
1. blue, 2nd
2. red, 1st
3. yellow, 3rd
4. green, 4th

Activity 96
YOU CAN IF YOU THINK YOU CAN

Activity 97
2. feet, bases
3. strikes, out
4. hits, no-hitter
5. innings, game
6. runs, grand slam
7. games, World Series
8. teams, American League
9. teams, National League
10. sides, home plate
11. balls, walk
12. weight, baseball
13. umpires, game
14. managers, team

Activity 98
1.	sharp	12.	lark
2.	shark	13.	bark
3.	share	14.	dark
4.	care	15.	dare
5.	chart	16.	date
6.	charm	17.	late
7.	hard	18.	lane
8.	hare	19.	cane
9.	fare	20.	cone
10.	farm	21.	done
11.	alarm		

Activity 99
1. Truman
2. Polk
3. Madison
4. Fillmore
5. Garfield
6. Taylor
7. Washington
8. Bush
9. Coolidge
10. Hoover
11. Grant
12. Pierce

Activity 100
1. Alabama
2. South Dakota
3. Lake Michigan
4. Connecticut
5. Red River
6. Nevada
7. Rio Grande River
8. Indiana
9. New Mexico
10. Mississippi River
11. United States
12. New Hampshire
13. Iowa
14. California
15. Oregon

Activity 101
Answers will vary.